"Combining a childlike ent   ith's
understanding of the natur   pla-
nations and insight into why it is important for us, not just the
specialists, to know such things as how cells get their energy. For
decades he saw the pursuit of truth through science as the height of
life's purpose. What could top the joy of scientific exploration? Sy
has an answer for this question too—discovering the God who created these wonders. As the book unfolds, he does not just show us
that science and faith are compatible. He offers the story of his life
to illustrate how the two together offer a new and much heightened
view of life's purpose."

PAUL WASON, vice president of life sciences and genetics at the
John Templeton Foundation

"An arresting, wholly transparent account of a scientist's struggle with faith. There are many books of this sort, but almost none
of this caliber or candor. Garte is a biochemist who competently
explores physics, philosophy of science, quantum entanglement,
mathematics, evolution, consciousness, and the fight for morality
and justice, all in a fast-moving personal story that's quite funny at
points and heart-wrenching in others."

PERRY MARSHALL, author of *Evolution 2.0*, and founder of the
Evolution 2.0 Technology Prize

"Sy Garte may be compared to C. S. Lewis in *Surprised by Joy*. As
his pastor, I delighted in reading this personal narrative about Sy's
transformation from an atheist to a believer in the triune God. His
conversion was stimulated by his thoughtful inquiries as a scientist
but completed by an encounter with the risen Christ. Sy found God
only to realize that our gracious God had been wooing him with
love and glimpses of joy for decades. A book worth reading by anyone who struggles with the intersection of science and faith."

REV. MARTHA MEREDITH, pastor of Rockville United
Methodist Church

"There are two pernicious myths about the Christian faith that circulate through modern culture. The first asserts that to become a Christian, one must park one's mind at the doors of the church before entering. The second myth is that senior academics set their foundational beliefs in stone early in their careers, and they remain intact until retirement. The spiritual and intellectual voyage of Dr. Sy Garte crushes both of these myths. Raised by parents steeped in communism and anti-theistic materialism, then educated in biochemistry and biological evolution, Garte spent much of his academic career as a fervent atheist. Yet an intuitive inkling that something was missing in his life—and in his science—opened the way for him to discover the grace of God in his Son, Jesus Christ. This book deals with many intellectually challenging issues Garte faced in his journey, including a renewed understanding of evolution as God's method of creation. Garte is a brilliant example of a Christian following Jesus's command to love God with our minds (Matt. 22:37)."

DENIS O. LAMOUREUX, DDS, PhD, PhD, professor of science and religion at St. Joseph's College, University of Alberta

"In *The Works of His Hands*, biochemist Sy Garte shares what he learned (and is still learning) during his career as a scientist in search of purpose and meaning. He discovered Christianity, to paraphrase C. S. Lewis, as the 'light by which everything else may be seen.' His insights, offered in narrative and creative storytelling, provide a road map for reconciling science and faith, both for spiritual seekers peeking over the fence from the yard of agnosticism and for worried believers gazing out the chapel window at the so-called challenges of modern science. Thoughtful, provocative, playful, and intimate."

STEPHEN O. MOSHIER, professor of geology at Wheaton College

THE
works
OF HIS
hands

THE
works
OF HIS
hands

A Scientist's Journey from Atheism to Faith

SY GARTE, PhD

Kregel
Publications

A portion of chapter 5 was originally published in "Teleology and the Origin of Evolution" in *Perspectives on Science and Christian Faith* (Boston: American Scientific Affiliation, 2017). https://network.asa3.org/page/PSCF?. Used by permission.

A portion of chapter 6 was originally published in "Evolution and Imago Dei" in *God & Nature* (Boston: American Scientific Affiliation, 2012). Used by permission.

ISBN 978-0-8254-4607-8, print
ISBN 978-0-8254-7584-9, epub

Printed in the United States of America
19 20 21 22 23 24 25 26 27 28 / 5 4 3 2 1

*This book is
dedicated to
the love of my life,
my wife,
Anikó Albert*

Great are the works of the L<small>ORD</small>,
[they are] studied by all who delight in them.

The works of his hands are faithful and just;
all his precepts are trustworthy.
—Psalm 111:2, 7

Contents

Foreword

THIS REMARKABLE BOOK documents a journey of personal discovery and intellectual exploration, ranging over some of the greatest questions we face as human beings. Science and religious faith are often declared (generally by those anxious to shut down any discussion of the matter as quickly as possible) to be incompatible. It's an influential view, though resting on an outdated understanding of how we make sense of our world. In this engaging work, Sy Garte takes us on a myth-busting intellectual journey as he tells his own story of discovery and reappraisal, raising questions about some of the most deeply entrenched cultural certainties of our time.

Garte is lyrical in his praise of the natural sciences and helps us capture the sheer sense of wonder and intellectual excitement that accompanies a respectful and loving engagement with the world of nature. The work is shot through with beautifully crafted vignettes of scientific description—such as the role of quantum entanglement in photosynthesis.

Yet Garte, while celebrating the explanatory successes of the sciences, is alert to their limits. For a start, there are deep questions about meaning and value that science cannot answer. Yet the problems go much deeper than this. Garte highlights some fundamental questions about the rationality of our universe that arise from an appreciation of its "uncertainty and strangeness." Can human reason really hope to grasp the complexity of our world? For Garte, the philosophical implications of quantum physics and the role of chance call into question the "pure materialism" that is so often—and so wrongly—depicted as the natural default ontology of science.

How can such a materialist philosophy—something that is bolted on to the scientific method rather than being its essential foundation—help us account for our emotional reaction to our world, expressed using rich words such as *beauty, magic, passion,* or *joy*? While still an atheist, Garte found himself wondering where all this "emotional stuff" came from. Was there a better way of understanding our world, which could accommodate these important experiences plausibly and naturally? Garte's moving and engaging account of his "call of faith" weaves together his growing sense of the limits of a purely scientific knowledge and an awareness of the imaginative and rational appeal of Christianity.

The Works of His Hands thus leads us through two territories. The first is the world of the natural sciences; the second is the world of religion. Many unthinkingly assume these are incompatible or in a permanent state of warfare. Garte's story will cause many to rethink this long-outdated media trope and to reflect on how science and faith might get along better. Garte hints at the great Renaissance metaphor of the "Two Books of God" as he explains the harmony he finds between the two books of God's revelation to humanity, the Book of Words and the Book of Works. This timely and well-crafted book deserves to find a wide readership, especially among natural scientists who are weary of the sterility and superficiality of the "new atheism."

ALISTER MCGRATH
Andreas Idreos Professor of Science and Religion
Oxford University

Preface

THERE IS A popular joke about a man caught in a flood who prays to God to be saved. He hears an answer to his prayer: "I will save you, My son." So with a glad heart, he waits for the miracle to happen. A boat comes by, and the people in it call for the stranded man to join them, but he says, "No, thank you. God will save me." And he continues to wait for the miracle. Two more boats follow (as in any good folktale), but his answer is the same.

The man drowns. When he gets to heaven, he confronts God: "Why didn't You save me like You promised?"

God says, "I sent you three boats. What more did you want?"

Here is another version of the story. Instead of a believer, our hero is an atheist. Caught in the flood, he thinks, *It sure looks like only a miracle could save me, but I don't believe in miracles, so I must save myself.* He dives into the swirling waters and tries to swim to safety. He sees a boat and hears people calling to him, but as a rational person, he knows that the chances of there being a real boat there just when he needs one are so small as to make such an occurrence essentially impossible. So he decides that the boat must be an illusion conjured up by his mind, and he continues swimming.

After he drowns, he also goes to heaven, where God asks him why he didn't get into the boat to save himself.

"Because it made no sense for there to be a boat there, and I used my reason to reject that possibility. Logic is stronger than belief in fairy tales," the man answers.

God smiles. "Yet here you are in heaven, in front of the real God who made you, as real as the boat that could have saved you."

God works through the natural world, and the natural world *is* the miracle.

The meaning of both parables is, of course, that God works through the natural world, and the natural world *is* the miracle. The first man expected an angel to come down, swoop him up, and carry him to shore. He rejected the possibility that an ordinary boat with a mortal human could be God's instrument of miraculous salvation. The second man assumed that his salvation was entirely in his own hands and rejected even the evidence of his senses that a miracle could happen. Some believers fail to see that the "mundane" world of nature, with its scientific laws, is itself divine—that is, flowing from God's will and character. They miss the miracle in everything around them, looking instead only to what they consider to be the rigid and unbendable Word of God. They share this blindness with many atheists who, like our second man, also find nature devoid of anything related to divinity, but they think of all reality as the rigid and unbendable consequence of arbitrary natural laws.

They are both wrong, of course, because God is not rigid or unbendable, and His laws of nature reflect this. The great gift of God to the universe is freedom. We see this when we examine the physical and the biological worlds in detail. God has created a universe in which the fundamental particles of matter have the freedom to exist in multiple states; it is only when they are observed that they make their "choice." As for life, God has created it in a way to allow a breathtaking diversity. There is freedom in evolution—freedom to explore, to succeed or fail. And God has granted His special creation of humankind the most freedom of all: freedom to make moral choices. To sin or to love; to worship or to scorn. To recognize that the boat is a miracle of salvation or to reject it.

My own salvation came through the understanding that the natural world—and its description by science—is a strong witness to God's existence and majesty. I did not reject the grandeur of this world as either too secular or too illusory to be important—I embraced it and devoted my life to scientific research. And that path eventually led me from atheism to faith (with a good deal of help from the Holy Spirit along the way).

In this book, I will try to show you how a belief in God the Creator should always be in tune with, and never opposed to, modern science. I will also tell you that matters of faith are not provable—and are not subject to proof in a scientific sense. This book was not written to convince anyone to adopt a certain set of beliefs. That is far from my interest. I have written this book more as a "guide to the perplexed" for people of faith (or open-minded atheists) who wish to embrace the modern world of science and technology and enjoy the intellectual and emotional beauty of science without giving up any part of their equally beautiful and soul-enriching faith in God.

As passionately as I try to follow the path of Jesus, and as fervently as I pray to God, giving thanks for His blessings in my life, I am equally passionate about the beauty and wonder of our natural world as revealed by the hard work, brilliant ideas, and beautiful synthesis of science. I find that these two passions are complementary and mutually reinforcing, and in fact may be two human definitions of a single unified passion, perhaps of divine origin.

My journey from atheism to Christianity was long and winding. I am telling it here because it might be of some use to those who find themselves wondering about the big questions of life. We will begin with some of these questions in chapter 1, which describes where

I started and how I discovered that questions are more important than answers.

The book is divided into two unequal parts. In part 1, I discuss how several scientific disciplines influenced me on my journey. Part 2 covers many of the issues and questions I faced once I had become a follower of Jesus Christ.

In chapters 2 and 3, I talk about some of the surprising and not widely known scientific realities that first got me thinking that the alleged dichotomy between reason and faith might not be real.

Chapter 4 is where I indulge my love for biology and attempt to explain how life works. The living activity in a tiny ribosome is a testament to God's magnificence on a par with the birth and death of galaxies. There is some technical detail in this chapter, although I have put more details in a technical appendix for those with special interest in the subject matter. Chapter 5 is devoted to evolution: what it is not, what it is, and how it works. Chapter 6 is about my favorite species: us. Human beings are special. Yes, I am an unabashed believer in human exceptionalism, and I will try my best to make a case for it in this chapter—or at least to thank God for being made in His image.

Throughout these chapters, I weave together the story of my growing awareness of God with my growing understanding of the scientific ideas that I was learning about at the same time. In chapter 7, I approach some of the philosophical ideas I discovered on my journey. I talk about the three great origins—the origins of the universe, life, and humanity—for which science cannot offer ultimate explanations. Chapter 8 is about the limits of science and the things we know that we cannot know scientifically.

Finally, in chapter 9, I leave science and talk in more detail about my own journey. This is the most personal chapter in the book, and it is meant to be read as one of many such stories about how Christ and the Spirit can move us to faith.

Part 2 begins with two chapters (10 and 11) that fill in some of the details about what happened when I became a Christian and how I sought and found answers to a whole new set of questions related to faith. In chapter 12, I discuss some of the controversies about evolution from a Christian viewpoint, explore the expanding new ideas in evolutionary theory, and have a closer look at the evolutionary creationist worldview. Chapter 13 provides a summation of where I am today as a scientist and deeply committed follower of Christ. Finally, chapter 14 is a short conclusion and a prayer of thanksgiving to our Lord and Savior.

I have included appendices with suggestions for discussion questions (appendix A) and further reading (appendix B), as well as one that provides more detail on some of the material touched on in chapter 4 for those with a deeper interest in biology (appendix C). There is also a short description of how I made an interesting discovery about Darwin while visiting the British Library in appendix D.

Science is distilled doxology.

Within the text there are four stories, written in the form of fables, that attempt to illustrate points I am trying to make in a (hopefully) amusing way. Some readers might feel that these fables are irreverent, or perhaps even verge on the sacrilegious—if that is the case, I apologize. Please know that I love God, and if I take any liberties for the sake of being a bit more lighthearted, this should not be taken as a sign that my devotion to the majesty of our Lord is less than profound.

To summarize in a few words what I am trying to convey: science discovers and describes natural laws, and natural laws come from

God. Science is distilled doxology. Now, let's start at the beginning and see where I came from and how I began to ask the questions that led me to begin my journey to God.

PART 1

Getting There

CHAPTER 1

The Importance of Questions

LIKE MANY FOLKS, I absorbed my first religion from my parents. It was an unusual religion for an American. It had nothing to do with God, but it was dogmatic, doctrinaire, and authoritarian. It had its own moral code, its own saints, and its own schisms. It was based on faith, and it suffered from a history of inherent contradictions and failures. It was communism.

My grandparents were Russian Jewish immigrants and revolutionaries. A granduncle fought in the Russian Revolution. Another granduncle founded the furriers union. My grandfather was a leading communist organizer in Boston who knew radical leaders like Nicola Sacco and Bartolomeo Vanzetti and helped found the upholsterers union. One grandmother was an important member of the International Ladies' Garment Workers' Union. My parents were card-carrying members of the American Communist Party in the 1930s and '40s. My sister joined picket lines for Julius and Ethel Rosenberg (who were executed as communist spies). I was briefly the president of the Students for a Democratic Society chapter of my college, and I participated in numerous marches and demonstrations for civil rights and against the Vietnam War. I was at the

Columbia and City College of New York campus takeovers by radical students in 1968 and 1969.

As for traditional religion, it was of course absent from my upbringing. I had no bar mitzvah at age thirteen. I never set foot in a synagogue, church, or temple, never attended Hebrew school, never celebrated any holiday except New Year's Day (which was condoned by the Soviet authorities as an acceptable time to give presents to kids) and of course May Day and Labor Day (in a quiet way). In December we had no Christmas tree, no menorah, no songs, no celebrations. I was one of the first kids in America to say "Season's greetings" instead of "Merry Christmas." In the spring, we avoided Easter egg hunts and never had or even attended any seders.

My parents quit the Communist Party just before my birth, but they remained committed to the political and anti-religious philosophy of Marxism and were strongly opposed to anything that smacked of spirituality or transcendence. They laughed at the idea of God. They were sure that there was no God; there could be nothing like God; God could not possibly exist. But they did not stop there. Like many of the modern anti-theists, my family thought of religion as not only wrong but evil. Religions were based on lies and had the explicit purpose of enslaving and oppressing humanity throughout history. My parents' atheism was indeed a deeply felt religious belief, and it was successfully transmitted to and accepted by me at a very young age.

Like all faiths, the faith I was born into raised questions. And like all faiths, mine had ready answers for most of these questions. Why are we here? What is our purpose? The answer to these were clear: to work for the betterment of all humanity, to strive for fairness and justice in the world for all, to defeat the evil forces of superstition, oppression, and hatred. Good answers.

But even early in my life, I sensed a problem with them. If there is no concept of fairness in nature, and if humans are nothing more than natural beings, why should they be fair?

Where did the subversive concepts of fairness and justice come from? What was their source if it wasn't from the natural world?

If there is no absolute moral standard, why is it important that there be no starving children, no families decimated by the ravages of capitalist-imperialist warfare, no slaves, no oppressed workers suffering from degradation at the hands of greedy, self-satisfied, oppressive capitalists? After all, aren't those capitalists simply acting out in extreme the pseudo-Darwinist prerogative of survival of the fittest? Justice and mercy were part of the background of my youth. "It isn't right that Negroes can't ride in the front of the bus." "Workers can't get justice." "It isn't fair that the colonialists take all the resources from the countries they exploit." But where did the subversive concepts of fairness and justice come from? What was their source if it wasn't from the natural world?

The answer I came up with was that humans had somehow evolved to a higher level in the midst of a cruel and uncaring world, that humans had evolved a sense of purpose and a potential for further growth and development. I felt that through an evolutionary quirk (what Richard Dawkins later referred to as a "spandrel"), humans had become a unique species of animal that could feel, think, and create. I understood that we humans had evolved from the natural world, but I also came to see that we were something more. We could create beauty, we could change our lives, we could love. But these were vague and uncertain ideas, pretty well lost in the maelstrom of anti-religious views that dominated my mind.

As a young man, I would never have thought that I could possibly become a theist. I subscribed to all the arguments against religion. I found the following especially convincing:

- If there is a God, why doesn't He show Himself or provide some evidence of His existence?
- Religion has been an evil force in history.
- A belief in the supernatural is irrational, not provable, and not falsifiable, and it is based only on unreliable subjective experience.
- The claims of Christianity—life after death, resurrection, and miracles—are magical and scientifically impossible; they violate the laws of nature.
- The Bible is a book of mythical fairy tales filled with bad science, bad history, and the terrible deeds of a jealous, angry god figure and his people.

These arguments have become even more popular today. One can find them from comedy sketches to the writings of academics and intellectuals, not to mention all over the internet. It took me a very long time to discover that they were all false.

Why Questions Count

What questions we ask can change the very way we see the world. I first learned about the importance of questions when I became a research scientist. All scientists eventually learn that answers are easier to find than the right questions. The best scientists are those who find the right questions (either through brilliance or luck). One can waste decades finding answers to questions that are not very important or interesting, whether they are about science or about faith. In my case, asking questions about the faith I grew up with— faith in Comrade Stalin—and the atheist worldview was critical to my being able to reject such ideas and search for better answers. Some of those questions are listed at the end of this chapter. But before we get to that, let's take a look at some of the critical questions in science that eventually led to a major revolution in how we think about the nature of reality.

There was a time in the history of science when many people thought that there were no more new questions to be asked—that almost every worthwhile question about nature had been answered. Phrases like "there is nothing more to be discovered in physics" and "all that remains is more precise measurement" reflect the sentiments of many scientists at the turn of the twentieth century. Albert Michelson said, "While it is never safe to affirm that the future of Physical Science has no marvels in store even more astonishing than those of the past, it seems probable that most of the grand underlying principles have been firmly established."[1] He went on to say that future work in physics will be largely filling in data on the "sixth place of decimals."

It was widely believed (with some dissension) that all of the basic theoretical understanding of the universe had been discovered. The final brilliant stroke had been the work of James Clerk Maxwell on electricity and magnetism. Maxwell's famous equations showed how these two mysterious forces were interrelated and how the concept of fields (magnetic fields and electrical fields) could explain the behavior of many physical phenomena, including light. The general view was that even if there were a few details to fill in (e.g., all of biology), it was clear that the scientific method had been successful in its attempts to understand nature. We were at the point of knowing everything.

There was, however, an important missing piece in the fabric of human understanding of nature: confirmation of the existence of the ether. The ether was believed to be an invisible, intangible substance that permeated space and was supposed to be the medium through which light traveled at such immense speed. At the time, scientists thought of light as simply a wave, and waves always require some medium in which to move. For example, water is the medium for the motion of ocean waves, and air is the medium for sound waves.

In 1887, Michelson and Edward Morley did an experiment designed to find tangible evidence for the ether. What they found, contrary to their expectation, was that the speed of light was the same regardless of its direction. This suggested that there was no ether, but it left the question of how light traveled unanswered. The speed of light had been measured and was known to be a constant. But without an ether to travel in, it wasn't very clear how light could be a wave. And if not a wave, what was it?

Einstein found the answer, but it was not something easy to grasp. The movement of light turned out to be an exception to everything known about relative motion. In our normal experience, if you are sitting on one train, and your friend is going in the same direction on another train on a parallel track at the same speed, you can wave and smile and hold up signs if you want, since relative to her, you are not moving. But if the train is going the other way, you have no chance of even seeing her, since her speed relative to yours will be double your actual speed. This is also true of sound waves and everything else that moves. But the speed of light is constant for an observer whether the observer is moving toward or away from the light. Why is light different? Einstein's shocking answer had to do with the nature of time. In fact, the truth is that the speed of light is always constant because time is not.

Einstein's theory of special relativity provided an explanation for the nature of light and time that lies outside of our normal experience. He proposed that time can slow down or speed up depending on how fast you move. I don't mean that an hour in the dentist chair seems to last much longer than two hours at the movies with your lover. What Einstein predicted was that if you put a clock on a spaceship and had it fly very fast for what was an hour on earth, when it came back, that spaceship clock would show that less time had passed, perhaps fifty-nine minutes, even less as the spaceship approached the speed of light. In other words, actual time itself, not our perception of time, literally slowed down on the spaceship compared to time here on earth. The idea of time slowing or speeding up is a principle of physics that defies our commonsense experience. But it turns out to be demonstrably true, confirmed by many experiments. For example, Joseph Hafele and Richard Keating showed in 1972 that clocks flying eastward on a jet lost time compared to reference clocks on the ground, while those flying westward gained time, as predicted by Einstein's theory.

The famous end-of-physics assessments by Michelson and others were wrong. The theory of special relativity was only the beginning of an enormous revolution in physics that transformed the way scientists view reality. This revolution has been slow to enter the public consciousness, and its philosophical implications have been only marginally addressed. The problem is that so many of the answers to the new questions being asked at the start of the twentieth century were not only strange but seemed to undermine reason, logic, and common sense—the very foundations of science itself.

When I first learned about relativity and quantum mechanics (see the next chapter), I understood that a lot of what I had taken for granted might not be true and that in fact there was an important question that needed to be asked: *Is our world a purely logical and rational place that is fully understandable by the application of reason?*

I had learned that the obvious answer to this question must be yes, as required by the strictly materialistic, philosophical naturalism I was brought up to believe in. But as I read and learned more about physics and other sciences, including my own field of biology, I began to see that the answer to this question might be no.

It's important to clarify that this question is not inspired by current gaps in knowledge. The facts that we do not know at this time how to prevent or cure cancer, or how gravity is connected with quantum theory, or even how to make a computer that does what you want it to do (instead of what *it* wants to do) are not part of this question. Think about all the things we did not know just a few decades ago and then learned using science. The question is not about what we do not know, but about the nature of what we *do* know.

Before we proceed with an answer to this question, I want to show you some of the other key questions that arose in my mind while pursuing my studies and then later during my career in science. None of them are especially original, and many scientists shrug them off when asked. I did the same thing for a long time. But at one time or another, they all came back to haunt me, and the search for their answers led me along one very particular path. Each is addressed in chapters 2 through 9.

Is our world a purely logical and rational place that is fully understandable by the application of reason?

Why does every answer we get from research into any branch of science always lead to more questions?

Why is complexity the rule in nature?

Why is biological life so complex?

Is evolution by natural selection the best theory to explain how life became so diverse and complex?

Are human beings special, and if so, how did we get that way?

How did the universe, life, and human consciousness arise?

How do we go beyond the limits of the scientific approach to understanding and knowledge?

Aren't science and religious faith opposites and enemies?

These questions mark the milestones in my journey. I did find some answers to these questions, and I am still finding more. It took me a long time to arrive at these answers, and I will chronicle that journey in the rest of this book. Some of the ideas that I now believe answer those questions came from my scientific studies or awareness; others came from my growing appreciation of nonscientific paths to knowledge and truth. None of them contradict any scientific principles, but many of them lie outside of science. This means that before I could make any progress, I needed to answer a question that is the converse of the first one I asked: *Can we learn anything about our world without using the methods, tools, and results of scientific investigation?*

I concluded that we can. To understand how I came to that conclusion, and to learn how I resolved the other questions, you will need to read on.

CHAPTER 2

The Irrational World of Modern Physics

Is OUR WORLD *a purely logical and rational place that is fully under-standable by the application of reason?*

Logic and reason are good things, and they have been of great help to humanity during our long struggle to climb from ignorance to scientific truth and a better way of living. But they go only so far when it comes to understanding the natural world. It turns out, much to the surprise of scientists like myself, who had been trained to believe that mysticism was sheer nonsense, that reality can be downright mystical.

I took physics and physical chemistry in college, and in the latter course, I learned about the Schrödinger equation, one of the basic building blocks of quantum mechanics. (I even got one of my very few As because on the final exam I somehow was able to use this equation in a way that impressed my professor, netting me a grade of forty-seven, the highest in the class.) I also learned the funda-mentals of Planck's theory of the discrete, noncontinuous "packets" of energy that he called "quanta" (plural of quantum; see below). But like my fellow students, I saw nothing of philosophical interest in this material. It wasn't until a decade or so later, when I began reading books like *The Tao of Physics*, that I began to wonder about what it really meant that reality was based on some very strange science.

Chance, Determinism, and Baseball Cards

There are a number of strange things about the universe that science has uncovered in the past century, and among the strangest is the behavior of the tiny particles that ultimately make up everything. These particles (like electrons and photons) obey different laws than the everyday objects that occupy the classical universe we are familiar with. Their behavior is stochastic, meaning that it is based on probability: no matter how much we know, we cannot predict their future behavior with certainty.

We think of tossing a coin as a good model for a random probabilistic system, but that is just what it is—a model, not a true stochastic system. The outcome of a coin toss is actually deterministic: if we knew everything possible about the way the coin is flipped, we could predict the outcome. I have personal experience with this kind of system, since my friends and I carried out (and replicated many times) very successful experiments on it when I was about twelve years old. We all collected baseball cards that came in bubble gum packages and were randomly selected, but some of them (like Mickey Mantle or Duke Snider) were much more valuable than others. So we played a game that allowed us to capture (or lose) these valuable cards from each other. One kid would flip a card into the air, which would land on the ground either picture up (heads) or down (tails). Another kid would flip one of his cards. If the second kid matched the result of the first card flip (heads or tails), he got to keep both cards. If he got the opposite result, he lost his card.

You would think that this would be a fair, random game of chance. It wasn't. After a great deal of practice (about ten times the amount of time I spent on doing homework), I was able to flip cards in a way that gave me the heads or tails I needed to win. I don't know how I did it, but it worked. In fact, we all were able to do it. I was able to flip up to fifty heads (or tails) in a row. The collection of baseball cards I amassed (later thrown away by my mother, as happened to everybody I ever met) was quite impressive.

Theoretically, the same thing is possible for coins or dice (though a lot harder, unless we cheat and load them). But not for electrons or photons. No matter how hard we work, no matter how precise our technology gets, we cannot predict the behavior of individual elementary particles. The reason we know that these particles behave in a very different way from anything we are used to seeing or touching is the development of a theory of physics about eighty years ago that was as strange as it was revolutionary: quantum mechanics (QM).

Quantum Mechanics

The turn of the twentieth century saw physics as it was then known overturned by several startling developments. Max Planck discovered that the only way to explain some kinds of radiation was to assume that energy could only be emitted in a noncontinuous way, as a series of packets rather than a stream. The size of these packets, or quanta, was equal to the frequency of the wave times a constant (later called Planck's constant, h). Planck found that the amount of energy in a wave was equal to any whole-number multiple of the frequency times h: it could be 1, 2, or 3 times that value, for instance, but not 2.8 or 3.1 times. In other words, reality at this level did not appear to be smooth, continuous, and infinitely divisible.

Soon after, Niels Bohr demonstrated that electrons in an atom could only exist at these same discrete quantum energy levels, and Einstein found that light energy also came in these discontinuous packets of energy. Quantum theory was on its way to revolutionizing physics and challenging the scientific philosophy of existence.

When these ideas were first proposed, most scientists found them disturbing. The idea of a noncontinuous universe seemed to fly in the face of everything that science had learned up till then. Space was assumed to be as infinitely divisible as the mathematics of rational numbers used to measure it. Newton's laws of motion and all the laws of chemistry and energy were based on continuity. Nobody could imagine covering a distance from one point to another without passing through all the points in between, or heating something without seeing a gradual rise in temperature through all degrees between the original temperature and the final one. But Planck and Bohr had found that that's exactly what happened on the atomic scale. An electron could move from one energy level to another one, instantaneously, without passing through all the intermediate levels on the way.

But that was only the beginning. As physicists began to explore the ramifications of the quantum model of the atom and what it meant for matter and energy, things just kept getting crazier. Among the facts this new physics brought out was one that even Einstein refused to believe for a long time: at the very small level of reality where the quantum rules hold, everything is truly probabilistic and not determined. In other words, randomness is the rule, not just an apparent effect of our inability to predict how a coin will fall.

Quantum theory revealed that particles like electrons and photons do not actually exist as fixed points in space and time. Before any measurements are made, a particle exists in a probability density, in several "superposed" potential states. Once an observation is made (we measure a position, determine a mass, or detect a velocity), one of the potential states becomes "fixed" as the actual state.

This quantum "observer effect" is not simply attributable to perturbations caused by the detectors or measuring devices. It is not, for example, that detectors that are placed at the end of a pathway interfere with the beam along its path. In 2000, an experiment was conducted that proved that the mechanics of observation is not changing the phenomenon. Instead, the observer is somehow determining an after-the-fact reality based solely on the act of observing.

Consciousness is a basic and necessary ingredient of reality.

Think about what this means. If observation is a critical part of existence, and the observer is either a conscious being or an instrument used by a conscious being that records or measures the system under investigation, then consciousness is hardly a murky and inconsequential quality of human (and possibly other animal) minds. Rather, it looks like consciousness is a basic and necessary ingredient of reality.

In his book, *Quantum: Einstein, Bohr, and the Great Debate About the Nature of Reality*, Manjit Kumar discusses the detailed history of the development of quantum mechanics: "It was Heisenberg, in his uncertainty paper, who first advocated in print the rejection of one of the central tenets of science."[1] The author quotes from Heisenberg's paper. Heisenberg asserts that the central tenet of science is this: "When we know the present precisely, we can predict the future." Heisenberg labels this statement as an assumption, not a conclusion, and states that the assumption is *false*. Not only that, but he claims, "Even in principle we cannot know the present in all detail."

This was a revolutionary statement, and as further work proved it to be true, the scientific view of reality changed forever.

Many other scientists have made statements that reflect the mind-bending philosophical implications of QM. Here are a couple of quotes from two of them.

It is a striking fact that almost all the interpretations of quantum mechanics . . . depend to some degree on the presence of consciousness for providing the "observer" that is required for . . . the emergence of a classical-like world.

—Roger Penrose[2]

In the beginning, there were only probabilities. The Universe could only come into existence if someone observed it. It does not matter that the observers turned up several billion years later. The Universe exists because we are aware that it exists.

—Martin Rees[3]

Quantum Entanglement

Quantum physics reveals other very strange twists in a modern scientific view of nature. In quantum entanglement, two particles are linked in such a way that their states cannot be described independently of each other—anything that affects one particle instantaneously affects the other one as well, even if they are light-years apart. This violates what classical physics calls the principle of locality: causation requires that something carries the influence through space from one object to the other, and since we know that nothing can move faster than the speed of light, instantaneous causation should be impossible. Einstein, disturbed by the implications, initially dismissed quantum entanglement as "spooky action at a distance,"[4] and others have called it "the God Effect,"[5] but it is real and demonstrable.

If you think all of this is crazy, you are not alone. The scientists who discovered and studied quantum mechanics agreed. Here are a couple more quotes.

It is no longer possible to make predictions without reference to the observer or the means of observation. To that

extent, every physical process may be said to have objective
and subjective features.

—Niels Bohr[6]

The *actual and individual object* of classical physics is
replaced by a more abstract kind of *potential and statistical
object.*

—David Bohm[7]

The world we experience, the world we can see and feel and
touch, is ruled by what we now call classical physics, or the world of
Newton. In this world, reason and common sense prevail: things are
what they seem, and they behave the way we expect them to behave.
But now we know that the submicroscopic world of atoms, photons,
and other elementary particles is ruled by quantum physics, which
requires an irrational kind of interaction or dialogue between the
particles, their surroundings, and the person studying them.

Fundamental Uncertainty Is a Certainty

Werner Heisenberg proved that it was impossible to determine the
position and the *momentum* of an electron at the same time. The more
precisely we know one, the less precise we can be about the other.
Heisenberg's uncertainty principle was the first blow to the idea,
gained after so many decades of relentless scientific progress, that
eventually we would be able to know everything.

If the quantum rules applied to everyday life, we would be in
deep trouble. Perhaps I wanted to take a ride, but there was no way
to know whether my car was in the garage until I opened the door.
And then I might see it there, or maybe I wouldn't—not because
of the vagaries of crime or perhaps a late night at a bar ending in
friends having to drive me home, but merely due to the deep, underlying nature of cars in garages. If I were lucky and my car were

there, I could get in and drive, but I would not be able to tell how fast I was going as long as I knew where I was. Alternatively, if I knew my speed, I would not know where I was. To make matters worse, I might suddenly find myself linked to some other person or object out there in the universe whose state of being directly affected what I did. I might suddenly stand up for no apparent reason, simply because a pangolin in southern China decided to lie down. And so on.

Such strange phenomena that are part of the reality of nature at the smallest and most fundamental level make it difficult to maintain philosophical materialism as the one legitimate way to view reality. You might ask, then, why so many atheists continue to worship at the altar of reason and logic. I don't know the answer, but I do know that few of those who do are physicists.

I was still a committed atheist when I first read about QM, the observer effect, and the uncertainty principle as a young adult. I was as badly shaken in my faith in rationality as were the physicists who heard about these new ideas from Bohr and Heisenberg in the 1920s. Not knowing much physics (beyond the introductory courses I mentioned), I couldn't grasp the mathematical logic behind the theories, but I wondered what all of this meant for my worldview. I had to reject some of the critical components of a comfortable theory of atheism. One was that the world was a rational place described by rational laws. I had discovered that the basic principles of modern physics, from relativity to quantum mechanics, describe a world of reality that seems irrational to us. If *imaginary* and *irrational* are truly critical adjectives needed to give an accurate scientific description of nature, how can the labeling of anything as imaginary or irrational (such as God) be an indication of nonexistence?

I also started to doubt that we humans can use our talents to eventually attain total and complete knowledge of everything. I was still an atheist, but I was no longer a smug and comfortable one. Science itself had opened cracks of doubt in my sense of certainty.

We might wonder why the universe was created with this kind of uncertainty and strangeness. We cannot know the answer, but maybe it was something like what transpires in the following fable. (Note: this story—like all the fables in this book—is not to be construed as actual or in any way serious theology, but only as a thought experiment.)

A Fable About the Origin of Chance

After many attempts, God finally made the perfect universe. Everything worked great: the stars shone, the sun was brilliant; plants and animals, birds and fish were everywhere; and humans were happily living in the garden of Eden. There was no sin, no death, no misery, and no surprises. God looked at His creation and saw that it was perfect.

But now that God had gotten everything right, including those pesky laws of physics with their infernal constants [see chapter 8], there wasn't much for anyone in heaven to do. Satan kept himself busy by trying to tempt some humans, but he had no success. They always smiled and turned down his offers. Apparently, none of them were very curious about the Tree of Knowledge of Good and Evil or interested in disobeying the Master of Creation.

As the years and millennia rolled on, not much happened. The snake kept running around like all the other reptiles, and the humans kept loving each other, smiling, and praising God. They also sang a lot and played with each other. One day, the archangel Michael was hanging out on earth, watching a small group of humans who seemed to be amusing themselves quite a bit. They had invented a new game where they would take different sized sticks and throw them around, and depending on how and where they landed, they did something or other, which often made them laugh. While watching, Michael saw that the humans apparently had no idea where the sticks would land. At first he found that strange, until he remembered that humans were not very smart and probably were not able to predict how the sticks would fall based on the precise configuration in which they were held, the wind speed and direction, and the force and direction of the throw.

None of this was a problem for Michael, of course, but then he was an angel. He envied the humans their excited anticipation and cries of joy or disappointment at the results of the game, and he wondered if he would be happier if he were more stupid. But then he had the germ of an idea.

"Satan!" Michael called out after returning to heaven. "I want you to hear something. I have had an idea."

Satan came over and said he couldn't wait to hear Michael's latest idea.

"Maybe we should ask the Boss to try out one more universe, different from this one."

"Different how? This one is perfect."

"Yeah, but it's so boring." And then Michael told Satan about the game he had seen.

"Yes, I have seen that also. They call it a game of chance."

"A game of what?"

"Chance. That means they aren't smart enough to calculate future events based on causation." Michael nodded, then pitched his idea: "But what if the Boss made a universe where chance was really real, I mean even for us?"

Satan thought about it. "You mean, no laws of physics? How else could you do away with determinism?"

Michael didn't know, but suggested they take the idea upstairs.

As it turned out, God (omniscient as He is) had been thinking along the same lines for other reasons that are beyond the comprehension of either the readers or the writer of this tale. Satan made the case for a world where random chance played a big role.

God liked the idea and began to think of a way He might do it. I don't know how long it took God to think of the answer because God is not that connected to time, so it's really hard to say. But at some point He called His angels together and said: "OK, I am going to try again. Let's see how it goes."

And that's how quantum mechanics were born.

As soon as the new universe was built, God looked at it with satisfaction. "Not perfect this time, but good."

Satan saw the two people in the garden and got ready for his latest temptation attempt.

"Will this one be different, Lord?" he asked the Boss. After all, God could see the future as well as the present.

God smiled. "Oh yes, it will be. And I promise you one thing: it won't be boring."

Of course, we have no idea why God designed our universe to be based on chance, but it probably had nothing to do with the plot of the fable. We do know that the world works, and although it is indeed not perfect, it is just possible that it works as well as it possibly could. We don't know how well a strictly deterministic universe would function, but God does (maybe because He tried it?), and that's my point.

Does the discovery of the uncertainties of QM mean that reason and logic have no place in science? Or is QM, with its mystical results and otherworldly conclusions, a sign that scientific thinking is dead or no longer useful? No, of course not. Quantum theory is good science, and our inability to "understand" it with our limited senses and intuitions meant for the world of everyday objects we live in does not mean it is not true or that science cannot account for it. It can, and it does, and it turns out that QM is demonstrably real and very important in that same world.

For instance, we are finding out that QM plays an integral role in one of the biggest mysteries in biology: the mechanism of photosynthesis. All life on earth depends on photosynthesis. It was the process of photosynthesis that gave rise to oxygen gas in the atmosphere, and without photosynthesis, animals would have nothing to eat.

In the past few years, experiments have indicated that it is because of quantum entanglement that photosynthetic bacteria and plants are able to convert light energy to chemical energy with sufficient efficiency to allow for biological growth. I will discuss photosynthesis more in chapter 4—I will only say here that part of the process involves the release of an electron that tries many possible chemical pathways simultaneously to find the most efficient way to achieve conversion to chemical energy.

This is quite remarkable. It suggests that quantum entanglement, far from being an esoteric property of particles in labs, is probably the most important physical phenomenon we know of when it comes to life. No entanglement, no people. If it is true that entanglement defies our notions of normal cause and effect and suggests the existence of phenomena beyond our ordinary human understanding, I think it is quite amazing that life on earth is totally dependent on the reality of this extraordinary, even "godly" effect.

Photosynthesis is not the only part of life that works according to a quantum design—so does inheritance. The quanta are the packets of information we call genes. We cannot predict how the offspring of two parents will appear, since the characteristics of the offspring will depend on the chance of which packets (genes) are passed to the new individual. Biology is ultimately based on the stochastic model that quantum theory implies. Even the sex of a child is determined by random chance based on transmission of a bundle of quantum genes in the form of a chromosome. Mutations (which I will discuss more in later chapters) are generally random occurrences.

By the time I finally understood the philosophical implications of quantum physics and the role of chance, I had pretty much jettisoned my belief in a pure materialism, and I found myself in a state of uncertainty (much like an electron) regarding my worldview. But before we get too carried away with the idea that everything in our universe is based on pure chance, we need to remember an important point. It is true that stochastic phenomena apply to individuals in a population or collection of organisms, particles, or human beings; however, in aggregate, for the entire population or collection, things are very predictable and deterministic. This is why even though we cannot say anything predictive about the motion of a particular gas molecule, we can describe the behavior of the gas in a container with great accuracy. The same holds true for rules that govern everything from electrons to ant colonies to human populations: chaotic behavior on the part of individuals becomes regular in large aggregates. And this is why we can formulate scientific laws.

But not always. There are some aspects of our world that defy simple solutions, even when dealing with everyday matters like ecological dynamics, the shapes of things, coastlines, and that pesky subject that affects us in so many ways—the weather. As we will see in the next chapter, science is just full of surprises.

CHAPTER 3

Science Surprises

WHY DOES EVERY answer we get from research into any branch of science always lead to more questions? Why is complexity the rule in nature?

As a young atheist, I studied biochemistry and found myself emotionally drawn to the beauty and basic order of science. The way cells work is so magnificent that learning about it always gave me a thrill. When I studied and later taught the mechanism by which proteins are made in cells, I always felt a chill down my spine. I was told once by a student that my voice, my body language, and my tone of conviction when I described how ribosomes, tRNA, and all the components of the process come together reminded her of a preacher filled with the Holy Spirit.

For many years as an adult, I worked at doing scientific research, and I felt philosophically at peace. I loved what I did. I was enchanted by the thrill of potential and actual discoveries. I felt that I had found my own comforting worldview, one that I thought was far superior to that of faith, since it had the advantage of being demonstrably true.

During this phase of my life, as I joined the academic scientific community, I loved the magic of creative thought. I loved the passion of the quest for truth and the overwhelming joy at finding answers that will stand as blocks in the immense edifice of knowledge that we human beings have been building for so long.

There was nothing dry or dull in my views of science. Note some of the words I used to describe the scientific process: *beauty, magic, passion, joy.* And although I was an atheist, I began to wonder where all this emotional stuff came from. There was no scientific theory I knew of to explain beauty, magic, passion, joy—or, for that matter, love, humor, music, art, thought, or creativity.

While in college and as a young adult, I began to see spirituality as one manifestation of the human attempt to reach higher in consciousness. I began to learn about consciousness expansion through enhanced mystical awareness. I was no longer worried that spirituality was too irrational or that it couldn't possibly be true, thanks to what I had encountered in the new physics. I didn't see spirituality as something outside of formal inquiry, but even if it was, I had already come to the conclusion that being outside of scientific investigation did not automatically make something unreal.

My mind was now open to new things, new ideas that were all around me. I loved the universal human goal of reaching for more: more enlightenment, more knowledge, more understanding and wisdom, more creativity and happiness. I recently heard the great theologian John Walton talk about this human characteristic, and his words reminded me of these early stirrings of the Spirit in my soul, long before I became a believer.

To be sure, these ideas were part of the culture around me—not the culture of my parents, but the youth culture of the times, which had rejected pure materialism in favor of a general interest in spirituality. Most of the people I knew were experimenting with things like Buddhism, meditation, mind-altering drugs—new ways of experiencing the beauty of natural reality. I didn't go that far (well, mostly

I didn't!), but I found all of it interesting and certainly not worthy of being dismissed out of hand. I did draw the line at ideas that were plainly not only outside of science but also anti-scientific—astrology, pyramids, various forms of magic, UFOs, and later a whole host of conspiracy theories and alternate reality constructions that I could tell were more flaky than spiritual.

I tried transcendental meditation. I looked into Buddhism. I tried a number of things, but nothing really clicked for me. And of course, I was still an atheist. I was seeking to fill the spiritual void in my heart and soul, but I didn't know how or with what. I found I simply could not accept anything on faith, since the whole concept of faith was missing in my worldview.

As my scientific research career developed, I began to feel that it wasn't faith that I had been missing but the thing behind faith: the human need to believe in something, to find a system of thought, a way of seeing the world and everything in it that was comforting, sustaining, satisfying, and indeed joyous. I had found this in science, so science became my method for reaching spiritual goals. The scientific revolution had transformed humankind and the world. Science had shown us how things work, including how we ourselves work. Science had let us see the truth and allowed individual scientists to feel satisfied in their quest and at one with nature.

> Complexity is not only the hallmark
> of biology but also the basis of a
> developing scientific revolution.

I expected that that was where I would stay in terms of my search for meaning and understanding. But more questions were arising all the time, and my journey was far from over. As before, the new questions were coming from my scientific milieu, partly from what I was reading about human psychology and consciousness and partly from the work I was doing as a biologist. I became fascinated by complexity. Complexity is not only the hallmark of biology but also the basis of a developing scientific revolution encompassing many fields of study.

Chaos and Complexity Theory

What would you say if I told you that you can use a computer to calculate something and get a completely different result every time you do the calculation? It doesn't seem possible, and yet it happened. In the early days of computing in the 1960s, a scientist named Edward Lorenz reran a simulation for a weather model he had done before, and he got a drastically different result, a weather pattern that didn't resemble the original one at all. How did this happen, when he used the same starting conditions? The second time, he rounded one of the twelve variables from 0.506127 to 0.506, but that wasn't supposed to make more than a trivial difference in the result. This made no sense and seemed to violate everything he knew about mathematics and science. But Lorenz did not check into a mental hospital or retreat into a cave—he kept looking into this phenomenon and came up with a name for it: the butterfly effect. He found that for some unusual iterative equations—equations used to predict how systems behave over time—the results can be so highly dependent on the exact initial conditions that the smallest change in those conditions can have huge consequences: a butterfly flapping its wings in Brazil could set off a tornado in Texas. The whole thing seemed chaotic, and that is the other name for the phenomenon—chaos.

We now know that chaos theory explains many very complex systems with highly interactive components. These include predator-prey relationships, the weather (which is why it will never be scientifically possible to make accurate weather predictions more than a few days into the future), the behavior of the stock market (which is why I am not rich), the way heart muscles work, and even how Christmas tree lights blink on and off.

Fractals

Closely related to chaos theory in terms of describing the enormous complexity of the real world are some very interesting (and beautiful) geometric structures called fractals, discovered by mathematician Benoit Mandelbrot in the 1970s. If we take apart a complex machine, we will eventually get to simple components like gears and bolts. That doesn't happen with a fractal object. The components that make up the fractal object exhibit self-similarity at all scales and are therefore just as complex as the original object—the complexity never ends, no matter how far into the details you go. It is easy to find beautiful examples of geometric fractals online, including the Mandelbrot set.

In the real world, there are very few perfect spheres, rectangles, squares, or straight lines. While we might think of a coast as a line (one dimension), it really isn't. The typical rugged coastline has a dimension that is greater than one but less than two (since a two-dimensional object would be a plane or a terrain). It is a fractal (named after its fractional dimensions), and like the mathematical fractals discovered by Mandelbrot, real-world fractals (sometimes called statistical fractals) are self-similar on many scales.

To visualize a typical fractal in the natural world, think of a rugged coastline like Great Britain's. From twenty thousand feet in the air, you would see a complex, roughly curving shape with bays, inlets, islands, and all kinds of features. Now imagine you descend to two hundred feet in a helicopter. You look down at a particular stretch of that coast, and it looks like it has the same degree of ruggedness as you saw from much higher up. Instead of large bays and inlets, you would now be seeing a portion of one bay, but you would still find features that looked like small bays or inlets. The coast doesn't get any smoother or simpler when you look at a much smaller section. Now, let's say you are on the ground at the water's edge. You will see small coves, channels, and rocks in the water. And it all still looks remarkably like the view from two hundred or twenty thousand feet up in the air.

Self-similarity is also found in clouds, trees, seashells, mountains, and galaxies; in lungs and leaves; and in DNA (discovered by yours truly[1]). Each of these can be expressed as a fractal, with a non-integer dimension.

Fractals and chaos are two aspects of the new science that has been called nonlinear dynamics or complexity theory. It governs heartbeats, sound waves, biological growth, and hundreds of other phenomena. So much of nature seems to fit a fractal model that I have entertained the idea that perhaps all of reality is fractal. This might be one of the greatest scientific discoveries of the computer age.

We now know that our universe is complex far beyond what we used to think. The universe is also fractal, since this complexity is replicated in our own galaxy, solar system, planet, town, house, body, individual cells, and macromolecules within those cells, all the way down to the basic particles and strings that somehow account for all matter and energy.

I think the best published work I have ever done, though it received little attention from the scientific community, is the first demonstration that the coding arrangement of DNA has fractal properties. It was published in the *Journal of Theoretical Biology* in 2007. When I was looking for jobs, I had people ask me, "What is this nonsense about fractals you have here in your CV?" because the work was (way) outside of my actual field. Oh well. It's still my favorite paper.

Is Simplicity a Virtue?

Many scientists believe as an overarching principle that the secrets of nature will all turn out to be understandable by means of beautiful or elegant theories—beautiful and elegant of course meaning simple and precise in science. Einstein was a key proponent, and $E = mc^2$ is one of the best-known examples of such elegance. The structure of DNA is another. But not all solutions are as simple and elegant as Einstein's equations or Newton's laws. Fractals are beautiful, but they are not simple. And they are much better representations of reality than simple geometry.

There is a famous story about the seventeenth-century mathematician Pierre de Fermat, who proposed a simple theorem and claimed to have proved it in an elegant way. His proof was never found, and the best brains of four centuries have failed to replicate it. Then in the 1990s, Fermat's last theorem was finally proven. But, exciting as this was to mathematicians, it was also disappointing because the proof was not at all elegant or simple—it was very long, complicated, and required highly specialized mathematics not known in Fermat's time. It could not have been *Fermat's proof*. Some people even think that Fermat did not actually have a proof, or that he must have got it wrong.

The simple, elegant solutions that scientists have traditionally sought are consistent with a materialistic view of nature. According to this view, everything we want to know can be explained using some basic principles, all of which can be expressed as natural laws. Furthermore, the expectation is that all this knowledge will make sense to us and be consistent with our sense that reality is logical and rational.

I too love the notion of a simple equation that explains a great deal. That is the holy grail of science, and it is a beautiful thing to come across such theoretical marvels. But as I learned about chaos, fractals, complexity, and other modern findings of science, my

doubts about pure materialism as the answer to everything grew
stronger. The realist in me saw the contradictions, the dead ends
and false starts, and concluded that the universe is trying to tell us
something, something that we haven't really wanted to hear: "Sorry,
guys, the easy stuff is over. Nice work with classical mechanics and
momentum and relativity and the Hardy-Weinberg equation and
Mendelian inheritance. Great stuff. But now comes the hard part.
And you are going to need a larger computer."

Or perhaps we're going to need a whole different approach to how
things work and how they came to be.

Fine-Tuning in Cosmology

What I learned about chaos and complexity helped remove my faith
in materialism, rationalism, and the other philosophical reasons I
started out with for not believing in God. But I also learned something that was more radical—something that actually made me
think of a Creator God as a rational idea, or at least as rational as
any alternative. This lesson did not make me a theist (that is still
to come), but it did suggest a positive *reason to believe* rather than
merely taking away *reasons not to believe*. That lesson was the fine-
tuning of the cosmological constants.

Most physical laws include arbitrary constants that cannot be
derived from theory but can only be measured experimentally—
they simply are what they are. I will discuss the unsolvable mystery
of the physical constants as an example of a hard limit on what we
can discover through science in chapter 8. But for a small subset of
these constants, the mystery has even greater significance. These
are the cosmological constants—the constants related to how the
universe was initially formed.

There are anywhere from six to about twenty of these numbers
(depending on different interpretations), and it turns out that their
values are highly fortuitous. If they were at all different (in some

cases by extremely small differences), our kind of universe couldn't exist, and neither could we.

According to modern physics, there are four forces that underlie all the physical laws of the universe. Two nuclear forces, the strong force and the weak force, govern interactions between particles within the atomic nuclei. At the other end of the scale of object size, interactions between large bodies such as stars, planets, and galaxies are dependent on the third force, gravity. Finally, magnetic and electrical forces between atoms and subatomic particles are different aspects of the fourth, the electromagnetic force.

The great goal of modern physics has been to find a unified theory that can integrate all these forces with each other and show how each force is related by some logical mathematical formulation to all the others. Some progress has been made. The weak force and the electromagnetic force have been shown to be interrelated; at a very early stage in the history of the universe (within the first billionth of a second of the start of the big bang), these two forces were actually one.

The relative strengths of the four forces are determined by specific equations that include some of the cosmological constants. Martin Rees, the distinguished British astronomer, writes in his book *Just Six Numbers: The Deep Forces That Shape the Universe* that these four physical constants (and two others) need to be exactly the values they are, or the universe would be radically different than it is. Changes in any of these constants would make stars, planets, and life impossible.

The fraction of the mass of two hydrogen atoms that is released as energy when they fuse to produce helium is 0.007 (0.7%). That is the source of the heat produced in the sun and in a hydrogen bomb. It is the amount of mass (m) that is converted to energy (E) in the famous Einstein formula $E = mc^2$, and it is a direct measure of the strong nuclear force. If the strong force had a value of 0.006 or less, the universe would consist only of hydrogen—not very conducive to the complexities of life. If the value were greater than 0.008, all the hydrogen would have been fused shortly after the big bang, and there could be no stars, no solar heat—again, no life.

As Stephen Hawking and Leonard Mlodinow put it in their book *The Grand Design*, "Our universe and its laws appear to have a design that both is tailor-made to support us and, if we are to exist, leaves little room for alteration."[2]

There are three possible solutions to the mystery of fine-tuning of the physical constants. One is that there is in fact a good theoretical explanation for these constants, and it will turn out that they had to be exactly what they are. This explanation would most likely be derived from the long-sought "theory of everything," which will connect gravity to quantum physics and answer all questions. However, the theory of everything has so far been elusive. The latest disappointing results from CERN, the largest particle physics laboratory in the world, cast further doubt on these expectations.[3]

Another possibility is that there are or have been an infinite number of universes. We happen to be in this one because this is the only one out of billions or trillions, each with different constants and characteristics, that we could be in. The multiverse theory is favored by many physicists, but it has the problem of being unprovable, since information cannot travel between universes.

The third possible solution, one that is not commonly considered to be within the realm of science, is that God created the universe in a way that allowed stars, planets, and us to exist. While scientists typically reject any supernatural explanations, it must be said that the God hypothesis is not any *more* removed from testing or scientific confirmation than the multiverse. Therefore, a rational thinker is free to choose between two equally plausible and equally non-provable ideas. I now choose God.

Back when I was learning that the world of nature is more mystical and irrational than I had previously believed, I had not yet chosen God. I didn't yet see any of that as pointing me to religion. It was simply showing me that there is more beauty in the complexity of life, mathematical structures, and everything than I had previously known. But this growing awareness of the truth I was learning from science did something important for my slowly awakening soul: it removed a barrier that I had long maintained, a barrier against the possibility of believing in anything that was not grounded in reason. The observer effect and quantum entanglement are not grounded in reason, and yet they are true.

The removal of this obstacle did not lead me directly to faith, but it allowed me to go forward when the time came. But before we get to that point in time, we need to explore in more depth the kind of science that I was not just learning about but doing as my career. And for that we will be diving into the messy, fascinating, and incredibly difficult world of the biological sciences.

Our planet is full of life. The significance of this fact is deep and wonderful. To begin to get an appreciation of the grandeur of life, we must follow, as I did in my scientific career, the path of understanding the amazing revelations of how life works.

CHAPTER 4

Wonderful Life

WHY IS BIOLOGICAL *life so complex?*

As a young man in graduate school, I studied the secrets of molecular biochemistry, read books and papers, and struggled with the mass of facts about chemical reactions, enzyme pathways, and cellular anatomy. But I also used to go outside, walk in a park, go to a forest or a seashore, and just look at the living nature around me. I would sit on a tree trunk in the woods and look down at the termites, worms, and insects swarming through the soil. A bird would call; squirrels ran past. For me, a city boy, this was all mysterious and beautiful. I used to sit for hours on the rocks on the coast of Maine, watching the waves and the small barnacles clinging to the rocks, waiting for each wave to bring its cargo of microscopic food. There were the seagulls calling and searching for food, the crabs hiding from them, and my favorite creatures of all, my fellow humans, going out to sea in their fishing boats, calling and laughing and loving. What a wonderful world this is, this world of life.

I started college as a biology major, but it turned out I didn't care for the subject—it was too oriented to premed students. I loved chemistry, which was much more of a problem-solving discipline, so I switched majors. But my first love was still the science of life—I just had no aptitude for remembering all the names of organs and species. So I decided I would be a biochemist and apply my love of chemistry to the study of life. And that, in fact, is what I did. After a bachelor's degree in chemistry, I went to graduate school, and throughout my studies and as I began doing research in applied biochemistry and molecular biology, the basic truth of biology was driven home to me time and again: complexity is at the heart and root of life. I will not attempt to define life here, because there are no perfect definitions—and besides, you already know what life is. But I do want to talk about the amazing ways that life works.

> This is a complex and intensely beautiful universe—one that includes monarch butterflies, blue whales, mockingbirds, birch trees, and, of course, us.

We know a lot about how living things stay alive, and we are constantly learning more and more. The lessons are similar to those from physics that we saw in the previous chapter: this is a complex and intensely beautiful universe—one that includes monarch butterflies, blue whales, mockingbirds, birch trees, and, of course, us.

All living creatures operate according to one universal scheme. While palm trees, beetles, and giraffes *seem* to have very little in common, the fact is that all life is based on a single universal plan. All organisms are composed of cells, tiny enclosed units of living material. If you were to look at living tissue from any kind of organism with a microscope, you would see the cells. Cells come in all shapes. They are like small sacks filled with material, surrounded by a membrane that separates the inside of the cell from the rest of the world. We know that before there were creatures made of many cells, all life consisted of single-celled organisms. The most common form of such single-celled organisms alive today are the bacteria.

A cell in your body operates much the same way as a cell in the body of an antelope or an oak tree or a germ that causes tuberculosis. The membranes that enclose the cells are water-impermeable (to some extent), and they form the barrier between what is alive (the inside) and what is not (the outside).

Chemistry

What happens inside living cells? A lot of chemistry. Life is really all about chemistry—the way molecules interact and react with each other. A chemical reaction is what happens when molecules change from one form to another.

When I was a child, my father gave me a chemistry set. I was very excited. I immediately took one of the bottles of chemicals (chosen at random) and dumped it into the large test tube. With only some trepidation (I was of course actually *hoping* for an explosion), I took another bottle and added its contents to the tube. Nothing happened. I shook the test tube. I added water. I added a third and then a fourth chemical. Still nothing. I was disappointed and, with a great sigh, resigned myself to read the instruction booklet.

The booklet revealed that, contrary to my own ideas, most chemicals don't usually react with each other. Only some chemicals will do spectacular things like change colors or explode or get hot or cold or produce new things like crystals, and that only happens if very specific chemicals are mixed in just the right proportions. Also, usually one needs to do all kinds of things, like add heat or an acid, and then wait a while. I was not impressed. But the lesson was an important one: chemical reactions are generally rare, slow, and unimpressive. We learn about the exceptions—chemistry sets and lectures are designed to showcase them. In the lifeless natural world, chemistry happens a lot less. There are of course chemical reactions that occur all the time in the oceans and in the atmosphere—when chemistry does happen, it tends to go on in gases and especially in liquids, not so much in solids (though that can happen also).

Chemical reactions happen most often in the liquid state because while molecules are free to move, they are not *too* free (as they are in a gas), so they have a better chance to meet up with other molecules and react. The best liquid for chemistry to happen in is water. There are many reasons for this. The molecules of water themselves can react with other chemicals. Also, water is a liquid at a temperature that is good for chemical reactions to happen. Other substances like ammonia, nitrogen, and things we usually think of as gases on earth are too cold as liquids to allow for fast chemical reactions. And, of course, the earth is full of water. We know that life began in water and that water is the most basic and crucial component of life.

In a world without life, chemical reactions are generally random, slow, and purposeless. In living cells, on the other hand, chemical reactions occur continuously. Thousands of reactions happen every minute in a typical cell, and they are nonrandom, very fast, and under well-regulated control. The speed of chemical reactions in living tissue is important. Most chemical reactions, including most of the ones that happen in cells, would normally take hours or even years to reach completion. But the same reactions in cells take a fraction of a second. In order to be alive, a cell must continually do things like build new molecules, manage energy, dispose of waste, find food, and divide and reproduce. If cells had to wait for hours for a single reaction to occur, life could not go on. Just imagine a factory where every task takes several years instead of hours or minutes. The factory would not remain viable.

Biochemistry and the Importance of Catalysis

So how do cells manage to complete the reactions that go on inside them so quickly? They use a chemical trick called catalysis. A catalyst is a substance that makes a chemical reaction between other chemicals go faster. The catalyst itself does not change; it isn't used up or turned into anything else. It acts as an agent, a helper. Since it remains after the reaction is over, it can play its role over and over again. The phrase "catalyst for change" is a good way to think of this. Imagine a person who helps get something done but isn't changed herself.

How do catalysts work? In most cases, they provide a platform for molecules to meet each other and react. The catalytic converter in your car is a familiar example from the nonliving world that uses metals to catalyze the reactions that break up pollutants. In living cells, the catalysts literally bring two or more molecules together, and they even supply the energy needed for some reactions. Cells use thousands of them, each hundreds of times more powerful, efficient, and specific than anything we have ever seen outside of life. These catalysts are usually enzymes, and they are made out of proteins.

Proteins do almost all the work in cells. Most proteins are enzymes, but others provide structural support to hold the cell together. Where do these proteins come from? The cell makes them. Each is a long chain of twenty different components called amino acids. The precise sequence of these twenty different amino acids gives each protein a unique ability and function. There are thousands of such proteins in even primitive cells. But how does the cell know which proteins to make, and how does the cell make them?

Genetics

The answer is in the genes. The instructions about which proteins to make are carried in the DNA sequence of each of the thousands of genes contained in every cell. There is a code, the genetic code, which translates the sequence of the DNA bases into the amino acid sequence of a specific protein. Each protein therefore has its own gene, and every gene codes for a specific protein.

The concept of inheritance of characteristics is an old one. We routinely say, "He has his father's nose," or, "She got her singing talent from her mother." Farmers have used selective breeding to produce better cattle, wine grapes, and other domesticated plants and animals. Genetics became a science well before anyone knew what a gene was made of. After discovering the role of proteins as catalytic molecules, most scientists thought that the chemical form of genes must also be protein. But in the 1940s, some clever experiments showed that what contained the genetic information in cells was not a protein at all but a very mysterious molecule called DNA (deoxyribonucleic acid).

DNA was mysterious because chemists and biochemists really didn't know much about its structure or purpose. Then in 1953, James Watson, Francis Crick, and their colleagues Rosalind Franklin, Maurice Wilkins, and Raymond Gosling solved the mystery. They found that DNA is a long, non-branching double chain (in the shape of a helix), to which are attached the four different chemical units, called bases, facing inward and interacting with each other. The bases are symbolized with a single letter: A, C, G, and T, based on their chemical names. Watson and Crick found that if the base on one chain was an A, the base on the other chain had to be T because a C, a G, or another A could not fit. Likewise, if the base on one chain was a C, the other chain had to have a G in that position. It was a biochemical jigsaw puzzle.

Their discovery meant that if you knew the sequence of bases on one chain, you could predict with certainty the sequence of bases on the other chain. It also meant that if the two chains were separated (like a zipper!), then each chain could produce a new double chain that was an exact replica of the first. Understanding the structure of DNA led immediately to a partial solution of the mystery of how genes work: how DNA can make perfect copies of itself and how information is transmitted from generation to generation.

The discovery of the double helix structure of DNA launched two decades of intensive scientific work in the new field of molecular biology, which revealed a picture of incredible beauty and complexity. We now know a great deal about the language that DNA uses to transmit information down the generations. Francis Collins called it "the language of God" in his seminal book by that title. The DNA language is a chemical language, which is coded and read by other chemicals following the laws of chemistry and physics—but also the specific rules of biology.

Among those rules, embodied in the genetic code, is the way the sequence of the bases in DNA is translated by the cell into the structures of proteins. Sometimes people confuse the genetic code with the gene or DNA sequence. The sequence is what distinguishes every organism from every other organism, and a gene is a part of that sequence that is translated into a specific "meaning" for the organism (see further discussion below), but all organisms use the same code—the same language, or system—that never changes. I won't go into a lot of detail here (it's easy to find information on the genetic code, and figure 5 in appendix C shows the code as a table). To put it very briefly: the code of life tells us that every three-letter sequence of bases in DNA signifies a specific amino acid in a protein.

All living forms replicate themselves. The DNA of every cell is precisely copied so that when a cell divides in two, each of the two new cells inherits exactly the same coded information in its genes that the parent cell had. But inheritance of the DNA sequence is only one part of how genes work. Genes have meaning. They mean something very different from their physical and chemical identity, just as the four symbols T-R-E-E mean a tall wooden plant, something quite different from the four shapes of those letters. Our brains can translate the meaning of the symbol TREE into an image of what it means.

DNA itself doesn't actually do anything. It is the repository for information, much like the information in this sentence lies in the sequence of the letters in each word. It is the sequence of the bases in DNA that holds the information. If you have blue eyes, it is because somewhere in your DNA there is a sequence of bases (such as AAGTTACGAATTCCCTGAAGCTGCGGTAACTTC) that holds the information for having blue eyes.

So how are the meanings of the genes translated if there is nobody in the cell reading the DNA message? We know the answer to that question: it is the existence of a beautiful (I would call it magical) translation system that converts the information in the DNA to make just the right proteins. For readers interested in learning more of the details, I have included a lot of the technical information in appendix C, and of course more can also be found in various online sources, including videos that show in varying degrees of detail the amazing process that converts DNA-based information into functioning proteins.

Energy

The translation system is not the only wonder of molecular biology. Life requires energy. There is an enormous supply of energy on our planet, more than enough to allow for all the things that living organisms can do—run, swim, fly, think, and grow. The source of that energy is the thermonuclear reactions that fuel the sun—the star that we orbit—and it comes in two forms: heat and light. The warmth from the sun allows life to flourish, since at colder temperatures the chemistry of life could not happen. But it is the *light* from the sun that powers almost all life on earth.

It isn't immediately obvious how living creatures can turn light energy into the chemical, mechanical, and electrical energy that they need to live. In fact, the process of conversion of sunlight into useful energy is at least as remarkable as the translation of nucleotide chemistry into protein chemistry.

Very early in the history of life, according to evolutionary biology, certain bacteria were able to capture photons of light in a chemical structure called chlorophyll. When a photon hits this chemical, an electron is knocked out and begins a long cascade of chemical reactions called electron transport. I mentioned the quantum physics of photosynthesis in chapter 2. But that's only part of the story.

Molecular biology infuses every living cell with what I like to call the holy breath of life.

When I first studied this process in graduate school, the details of these reactions were not well understood. We now know that in addition to electrons, photosynthesis uses protons that collide with and turn a protein molecule that resembles a wheel. This tiny protein wheel is part of an amazing enzyme called ATP synthase. As the wheel is turned by the protons, another part of this enzyme is moved by the turning wheel in such a way that a molecule of ATP is formed. In other words, the light energy is converted into the mechanical energy of the moving wheel, which is then converted into the chemical energy of the ATP molecule. And almost every energy-requiring chemical reaction or process in the cell uses the chemical energy of ATP. It is the common energy currency of all life.

Just as for protein synthesis, there are some wonderful online videos that illustrate the way ATP synthase and photosynthesis work. Be prepared to be impressed, if not amazed, as you watch these videos.

I will not go into any more detail about the other astounding ways that molecular biology infuses every living cell with what I like to call the holy breath of life. The subject is vast and it really does require a PhD and years of postgraduate study to fully absorb it. Just think of how the eye can see, how the nose can smell, how our nerves work with our muscles, how oxygen is transported and used to make energy (since we cannot photosynthesize, we use oxygen to make our ATP), how organisms consist of billions of cells all working together, and you will begin to get a small idea of the enormity of life's biochemical wonders.

But we don't need to know all the molecular details to appreciate this wonder. Not all biology is molecular biology and biochemistry (it's just that as a biochemist, I am somewhat slanted in that direction). We can look at life as it appears in front of our eyes, watch creatures from bacteria to whales, and see everything we need to see in order to understand the majesty of life.

What lessons did my growing understanding of the beauty and complexity of biology teach me? I learned that there was a deep principle buried somewhere in the natural universe that must be the source for the wondrous nature of life. When I first studied the details of the process of biological translation from coded information in DNA to the structures of proteins, I was struck by a sense of wonder that was new to me. I felt that I was being shown a mystical secret, a window to a hidden world of knowledge about life and the universe. I found it amazing that I had earned the right to learn about all of this, and I was excited and inspired to try to learn more, more than was even known at the time. At that point I made the decision that was to steer the rest of the course of my life. I would devote my life to the pursuit of unlocking all the mysteries of living beings; I would be a research scientist. And so it came to pass.

This also began the decades-long period of my conviction that the pursuit of truth through science was the height of life's purpose. I felt that whatever spiritual or mystical cravings I had experienced till then could be satisfied by my study of the secrets of biology. Among other subjects, I studied the theory of evolution and found the profound and simple truth of how complexity and beauty can arise in living organisms by Darwin's theory of evolution by natural selection.

CHAPTER 5

There Is Grandeur—Darwin's Evolution

Is EVOLUTION BY *natural selection the best theory to explain how life became so diverse and complex?*

At some point during my early adulthood, I discovered Charles Darwin. The first book of his I read was an old edition of *The Voyage of the Beagle.* It is a (mostly, but not only) scientific diary of that famous voyage, a wonderful read. At the time of the voyage and while writing the book, Darwin was not yet thinking about evolution. He wrote about his observations on the geology, biology, and people of South America. I then read Darwin's autobiography, several biographies, and the collection of letters published by his son. I eventually read *On the Origin of Species* and some of his other great works.

What originally drew me to Darwin was not so much his work as his life. Living in the countryside with his family, spending his days in his study, reading, thinking, measuring, and writing, Darwin was the quintessential scientific man of leisure. In his novel *The French Lieutenant's Woman*, John Fowles makes it quite clear that the nineteenth-century British scientist was usually a wealthy

gentleman who had no need to earn a living. Darwin was wealth-
ier than most and never had any financial worries. Science was a
hobby for him, one that many aristocrats and upper-class men of
good education and breeding indulged in, much like foxhunting or
raising orchids.

Of course, my initial view of Darwin was not quite accurate. His
life wasn't all a bed of roses: he suffered a great deal from a mysterious illness and was devastated by the death of his beloved daughter.
But it is true that he had the leisure to allow the brilliance of his
mind to shine forth. I was familiar with the joy that new ideas can
bring, even ones substantially less brilliant than those of geniuses.
The famous eureka moment (which I have been lucky enough to
have had on a couple of occasions) is really a joyous experience. It is
what almost all scientists live for. It is the reward for years of struggle, frustration, failure, and despair.

Darwin is of course one of the founders of the theory of evolution by natural selection. As it happened, almost exactly the same
idea was proposed at the same time by another, lesser known naturalist named Alfred Russel Wallace. The two men became friends
and colleagues rather than competitors and maintained a lifelong
correspondence (see appendix D).

We know from Darwin's journals and biographies that he
developed his theory over many years. He used many sources: the
biological samples he gathered and the notes he took during the
voyage of the *Beagle*, mostly in the Galápagos Islands, as well as
his knowledge of botany, zoology, and the way breeders used artificial selection to improve the quality of crops and livestock. He also
read widely, and we know that one of the immediate triggers of his
ideas was his reading of the works of Thomas Robert Malthus on
the limits to population growth. It appears that all these sources
slowly gelled into a theory that he tested on his own samples, taking
careful measurements and compiling a great deal of data. Darwin

was extremely careful and very slow to jump to conclusions. He believed in being methodical and precise, and he was in no hurry to announce his findings or his theory until he was sure it all made sense and was consistent with his data. Darwin wanted to explain the enormous diversity of different species found on our planet. Had these species always been there? Many people thought so, but others had doubts. There was a school of thought that new species had developed over time, that some species (like the dinosaurs) had gone extinct, and that evolution was a reality in biology. But nobody knew how or why it happened. Darwin didn't invent evolution. What he did was present a coherent and testable theory for how evolution works.

This chapter is about my personal introduction to evolution as a scientific theory, and the questions evolution raised that continued to lead me toward faith. In chapter 12, I will discuss controversial aspects of evolution and contemporary debates about the science of evolution and biblical interpretation. There are many excellent books, articles, and online sources on evolution and natural selection, so I will not go into great detail here, but I do want to make two or three points that are worth stressing, especially about what the theory of evolutions says, and—even more importantly—what it does not say.

What Is Evolution? (And What It Isn't)

Evolution is a form of change, and change is a universal feature of our universe. Stars form and explode, planets collide with asteroids, black holes absorb huge amounts of matter, and galaxies move farther from each other. On our planet, change has always been the rule: changing climates, changing atmospheres, changing landscapes. When Darwin looked at natural history, he saw change as a key feature of geology and biology. Species went extinct and habitats changed. Darwin used his observations of living forms and his knowledge of man-made changes to plants and animals to propose his theory: the evolution of life based on natural selection of the most fit variants among a population. Darwin had no idea how variation arose, or how characteristics that allowed for increased or decreased relative fitness could be passed down from one generation to the next.[1]

Not all change is evolutionary change. Various proto life-forms, modern crops, human culture, and the geography of the planet might have undergone substantial change, might even be said to have evolved, but none of these examples of change follow the strict definition of evolution. Evolution is very good at explaining the biological diversity of living organisms on earth. It cannot explain the origin of life, the existence of good and evil in human beings, or how technology changes. It cannot explain human sociology or psychology, the solar system, or why there are so many galaxies. Evolution is not relevant to the weather, the stock market, the collapse of Myspace, or the rise of Instagram. It says nothing about why there are earthquakes, floods, or two feet of snow on my driveway. Evolution is not related to probability theory, software engineering, physics, logic, information theory, error propagation, chemical equilibrium, or the writings of Plato.

Some people believe that evolution claims to be behind much of the above. It doesn't. It is a very successful theory about how natural selection links changes in an organism's genes (genotype) with its inherited characteristics or traits (phenotype). In other words, biological evolution is about biology, and biology only. This is not to say that culture and technology don't evolve—they do. But the way they evolve is very different from how biological evolution operates.

Biological evolution is a unique mechanism not found outside the biological world. What Darwin knew as artificial selection makes use of some aspects of the process, but not all of it. Darwin's concept of evolution only applies to biological change in the absence of human will, and only living entities with DNA and protein enzymes can evolve according to classical Darwinian evolution.

Darwin and the other early evolutionists amassed lots of data and evidence for evolution by natural selection, but it wasn't until our modern understanding of molecular biology that the detailed mechanism of how biological evolution works became clear. Some have claimed that evolution by natural selection is an unproven theory based on speculation and guesswork and that it has never been observed. That was partially true when Darwin proposed it. It became less true as more and more fossils were found and other aspects of animal diversity and history were studied, and even less true with the discovery of genetics and the basic mechanisms of inheritance and mutation. We have a huge amount of data showing exactly how major changes in genetic sequence have resulted from progressive, minor changes, first within a species, then between closely related species, and then further and further apart. We can follow the changes in the structure of genes from species to species. For example, in some cases, genes that were once functional become nonfunctional due to mutations. (These "fossil" genes are called pseudogenes.) There are also cases where a particular gene is broken in a specific way in species A, and all the species that are presumed to have evolved from it have the same break in that gene, whereas other related species that branched off from an earlier ancestor of A do not have that feature. One example is the loss of the GULO gene, needed to make vitamin C, in primates, including humans (see appendix C). In other words, when we say that there is evidence for evolution by common descent from genetic data, we mean very specific data that could only be found if the species we are looking at were derived from a common ancestor.

One cannot understand any part of biological science without understanding natural selection as the underlying basis of genetics, zoology, botany, medicine, physiology, and their related fields.

There is no scientific controversy here. The controversy is only a theological one—and as we will discuss in chapter 12, even the theological controversy is not hard to resolve in favor of the theory of evolution.

How Evolution Works

Evolution by natural selection is a complex and quite wonderful molecular process that requires a host of specialized biomolecules. The heart of evolution is a tight linkage between inheritable genotype and the gene-directed phenotype. This makes the phenotype the target of selection imposed by the environment and allows for advantageous genetic mutations to be passed down, increasing the fitness of subsequent populations, eventually creating new species and increasing adaptation of living beings to their surroundings.

Natural selection acts on the phenotype, but only the genotype can be passed from one organism to its progeny by biochemical means. This is why there must be a connection between genotype and phenotype in all life-forms. In modern, evolvable life, when an organism inherits a particular genotype, it also inherits the corresponding phenotype that is produced (or coded for) by that genotype. This is an essential characteristic of evolution by natural selection. Once a cell that can connect genotype and phenotype in this way exists, it can begin to evolve, but until we have such a cell, no evolution is possible.

The definition of evolution used by scientists is "a change in allele frequencies in a population over time." In order to understand evolution, we must understand alleles. In the previous chapter, I said that every gene has a specific sequence, and that sequence is what codes for a protein. And that is true. Mostly. (There is a lot of biology that is *mostly* true.) While different individuals of the same species have the same sequences—the same genes—they do have small differences in these sequences. This is true for humans too.

You and your friend have a very small number of differences in the exact sequence of most of your genes. In a DNA sequence of a few thousand bases, she might have a T where you have a C. This doesn't mean one of you is a different species—it would take a much larger percentage of changes in gene sequences to say that two organisms are from two different species.

These tiny gene sequence differences between members of the same species are called alleles. Some genes have many different alleles in a population; others have only two or three. In the whole population, the frequencies of the different alleles can vary from less than 1 percent to over 99 percent. In many cases, the different alleles have no effect on the gene or the protein made by the gene; in other words, the phenotype does not change. In other cases, they do. These effects might be small and not noticeable, but they can also be apparent, like differences in eye color, body size, bone structure, strength, tolerance to alcohol, susceptibility to disease, and so on. The existence of different alleles for genes is the reason people are different from each other. They are the molecular explanation behind the variation that Darwin observed, and they are often caused by mutations.

In any population of animals, individuals will undergo many mutations, genetic recombinations, and rearrangements, with the result that their offspring will have different alleles for many genes. When different alleles produce a difference in phenotype (such as longer hair or larger bones), they might result in a difference in the fitness—the ability to survive and reproduce—for that individual. Whether the change is for better, for worse, or neutral depends on the environment. Longer hair would be beneficial in a cold climate and detrimental in a hot one, for example.

When they first occur (and for thousands of years afterward), the result of these sequence changes caused by mutation is not evolution but increased variation. If the changes do not have any negative impact on the fitness of the organism, they will probably be passed on for many generations to some proportion of the members of the species. And then something happens. The climate changes, a new predator appears, an old predator goes extinct, a new food source is available. Now those individuals who have an allele that codes for a slightly different phenotype (maybe a lighter coloration or a slightly larger beak) *do* have a selective advantage. The key to evolution is variation. The more variation there is in a species, the better are the chances for survival in the face of environmental change.

But for life to persist, there must also be stability, and there is a balance between stability and variation. In fact, the balance is tilted heavily on the side of stability. Mutational errors are strongly guarded against by a number of complex enzymatic systems whose role is to repair mistakes in DNA replication. Most mutations are neutral with respect to their effects, and a very small percentage of mutations are beneficial. There are many more possibilities for harm than for benefit with any mutation. Some mutations are so lethal that they are never seen, since the new organism is not born. Some mutations allow for life but then cause disease later (cystic fibrosis, Huntington's disease, etc.).

For multicellular organisms, mutations are not the only source of variation. There is a mechanism called crossing over or recombination that occurs with sexual reproduction (yes, sex is good, not just fun!) and produces far more variation than mutations. This is why children might inherent different traits from each of their parents. Selection can then favor certain of these recombined genetic patterns and can lock them in the population. Of course, the reason that the two parents have slightly different traits in the first place is because they have different alleles for the same gene, and each child inherits only one of these alleles from each parent. And alleles, remember, are produced originally by mutations.

Why is there variation among individuals within a species in all living forms? We could easily imagine a world where all members of the same species were exactly the same (like identical twins or clones). The same height, eye color, and hair color, all the genes in our bodies in exactly the same form. We would all have the same reactions to drinking alcohol, the same allergies, the same eyesight, memory, or ability to carry a tune. We would thrive in the same environment and succumb to the same diseases, and there could be no evolution. But this is not the way it is—not for us, not for howler monkeys, elephants, oak trees, hammerhead sharks, or any living species.

Variation by mutation is easily explained by less than perfect accuracy when DNA copies itself. Since variation is essential for evolution, the optimal fidelity of replication cannot be 100 percent. If life always made perfect copies of itself, there would be no variation and no evolution. But too much variation would also be a problem for evolution because the property of inheritability would be damaged. If the accuracy of the copying were really bad, with lots of errors, then the offspring of a cell would not resemble the parent cell very much, making natural selection impossible.

Descent with Modification

A key word in the scientific definition of evolution given earlier is *population*. No individual animal or plant evolves—only populations do. As long as the population remains together, enabling random mating, there is an equilibrium of the allele frequencies (called the Hardy-Weinberg equilibrium), and not much change goes on. It is, however, possible for a highly favorable allele to arise, and though this happens rarely, when it does, it is likely to spread through the whole population. A genetic change producing a new allele that gives an important advantage to an individual (like better eyesight or stronger muscles) will make it more probable that that individual will survive long enough to have offspring that also inherit the same allele. These offspring also have a better chance at survival, and so on, until the entire population are descendants of the individual animal that had the new mutation.

But this is not all there is to evolution. If the animal is a bird, and the mutation allows for better eyesight, then we might soon have a population of birds with better eyesight, but they would still be birds. To see how evolution really works, we will use a hypothetical animal, maybe one in the cat family. Let's call it a lipard. And let's say that there is a population of these large catlike carnivores living on a large plain with plenty of prey animals. The lipards have gotten better and better at hunting thanks to several alleles in genes for vision, muscle strength, digestion of meat, and other traits. And all these alleles are shared by the whole population.

But now the population of lipards becomes divided so that there are two groups of lipards that cannot interbreed. Perhaps one group crossed a river, a desert, or a mountain range and couldn't get back, or they just wandered so far away that it wasn't convenient to find mates in the other group.

Now both groups of lipards continue to accumulate new alleles through mutations, but because they are no longer interbreeding with each other, the new alleles in one group do not spread around in the other group. With time, each group begins to differ in their alleles. Some of these differences might have arisen just by chance (genetic drift), not by adaptation or selection. The neutral theory of evolution holds that in fact most evolutionary change occurs by genetic drift rather than adaptation.

Because the two groups of lipards now live in slightly different environments, there could also be allelic differences between the two populations due to selection. Either way, the collection of alleles in one group will not remain the same as in the other group for very long. With the passage of time, some of these alleles will produce slightly different traits in one of the groups that are not found in the other. Both groups continue to change independently of each other, and after a long enough time, neither group resembles the original lipards. One group has become lions, and the other has become leopards. They still have a lot in common, but they are now two separate species. Please note that no lion turned into a leopard or vice versa. Both lions and leopards share a common ancestral species, the lipard, which now no longer exists. It didn't go extinct—it evolved. Lipards themselves had evolved from an ancestor that they had in common with tigers and snow leopards, and even further back with cheetahs and domestic cats. And they all became separate species the same way: population isolation, separate allele changes in the separate populations, and continued evolution by natural selection. This is what Darwin observed among species of finches in separate islands of the Galápagos chain.

We can keep looking backward in biological history. All the cat-like animals are descended from a no-longer-living ancestor shared with bears, wolves, hyenas, badgers, and other carnivores. If we keep going, we will find a common ancestor for all mammals, and then all vertebrates, and so on. For an excellent book that describes all of this in beautiful detail, there is nothing to match *The Ancestor's Tale* by Richard Dawkins.

Is there any evidence for this scenario of how the diversity of life arose? Yes, tons. There is so much evidence, both from fossil records and from genetics, that there is no doubt at all that the theory of evolution is correct. There was a time when it seemed that the fossil record had large gaps and there was a dearth of transitional fossils. But that is no longer true. We now have a wealth of animal and plant fossils that paint a coherent picture of the complex web of life throughout biological history. I will mention two examples.

In 2004, skeletons of an extinct fish with fascinating features were discovered in northern Canada. This fish had the flat head of a crocodile, and its fins had bones that would allow it to walk. It soon became clear that this "fish" (named *Tiktaalik*, an Inuit word for "fish") was a transitional fossil between fish and the first land-dwelling vertebrates.[2]

The evolution of whales is a complicated story, well documented by many fossils. Whales (cetaceans, including dolphins) share a common ancestor with hippos, and the fossil record shows the progression of many extinct species from a land-dwelling animal to many versions of aquatic animals that look more and more like modern whales. There are no major gaps in the evidence of how an ancient animal evolved into both modern whales and hippos.

There are still many unanswered questions on the details of evolutionary mechanisms. Some of those are discussed in chapter 12.

Is Evolution Really Without Purpose?

When I was first learning about evolution and reading Darwin, I was an agnostic regarding God, and I had no trouble accepting that evolution is true. I certainly had no belief in the separate creation of each species by God. But when I fully comprehended the incredible beauty of evolutionary mechanisms, especially the translation system, I found myself asking scientifically forbidden questions: Why? Why did life evolve? Is there a purpose or direction to evolution? Is it all just based on chemical accidents?

> I found myself asking scientifically forbidden questions: Why? Why did life evolve? Is there a purpose or direction to evolution?

The idea that evolution is blind, with no purpose or direction, is not consistent with a Christian view of an actively creative and omnipotent God. For scientists of Christian faith, it thus becomes important to determine if purpose (or teleology) is part of the evolution of life. The scientific mainstream has been opposed to this idea for a long time, and many have written that the idea of purpose is contrary to the very fabric of Darwinism. I was firmly in that camp in the past, and I even wrote essays about how the appearance of purpose is an illusion and how chance events and selection can explain such appearances. Now I believe that there is a good case to be made for the role of a directed purpose in the progress of life—a case based on our scientific knowledge of the origins of evolution.

While evolution is blind, teleology (defined as goal-oriented, purposeful action) is clearly present in the biological world. Some animals, including us, do indeed act with purpose—something that even atheist philosopher Daniel Dennett agrees with.[3] But I would go further and state that I believe the root of purpose in life is built into the central, deepest biochemical essence of evolution. It is therefore inevitable that what we see as teleology will arise as a result of evolution, even though evolutionary actions themselves are dysteleological. I suggest that for evolution, purposeful reasons are represented by the genetic code.

The central theme of the origin of evolution is about chemistry becoming biology. For that to happen, early life had to solve a very difficult chemical problem: to take one chemical system (nucleic acid chemistry) and have it interact with and provide information to a completely different chemical system (protein and amino acid chemistry). After that challenge was met and biochemistry emerged, life as we know it today could begin to evolve and function.

When we speak of this genotype-to-phenotype conversion system, we have left the world of organic chemistry behind. Of course, the detailed mechanisms of each enzymatic reaction still follow chemical rules. But the underlying feature of this system is not based on chemistry but on purpose. The existence of a genetic code is the very embodiment of teleology. The code exists as a means to an end, and the end informs the code. The genetic code and the protein synthesis machinery are inherently purpose-driven, which is manifested by the technical name for this process—*translation*. Any translation, whether it is from one language to another, or from an obscure code to a meaningful statement, or from an observation to a conclusion, is by its nature teleological. Translations do not occur spontaneously, accidentally, or by random chance. The translator has a purpose: namely, to convert some information into something else.

What makes the biological translation system especially teleological? After all, no living creature, not even us, consciously communicates any willful commands to any of our cells to make a particular protein, and there is no Aristotelian final causation of the function of the genetic code. If I am not arguing for a conscious will in the creation of this system, then where does the concept of purpose come from? As I wrote in an article in *Perspectives on Science and Christian Faith*, "Cells do not see the future and do not decide to change based on what is needed. And that is the point. Cells do not *need* to see the future, because evolution provides a way to deal with any novel circumstances or challenges in the absence of sight, thought, will, or any form of consciousness."[4]

Another way to look at the teleology that pervades biology is that it comes from some intelligence. With evolution, it might be considered an intelligent designer. This would imply that all life—not just us, dolphins, and chimps—is intelligent. At first glance this idea seems absurd. How could bacteria, fungi, or even jellyfish be intelligent without brains? I recently found a blog post by my friend Perry Marshall (author of *Evolution 2.0*) entitled "Are Cells Intelligent?"[5] When one discovers the amazing ways that bacteria, fungi, amoeba, and other "simple" creatures communicate, behave, and function, it is hard to deny some form of intelligence operating. For example, some bacteria can sense the presence of other cells of their own species, and they can form special structures able to send out spores when food is scarce and the population is large. The spores (like seeds) will allow the species to survive even if all the cells die of starvation.

I have called this "intrinsic biochemical intelligence," and I propose that it derives from the highly complex control and regulatory mechanisms within the cell. These include gene expression regulatory networks, signal reception for intercell communication, and interactions with the genome.

This sort of cellular intelligence is not conscious, but it is probably behind the evidence of purpose that we find in all life, including the teleology behind evolution. Evolution by natural selection is the cellular biological alternative to survival by conscious struggle. The translation system provides the nonconscious will to survive in all terrestrial life through evolution. That is its *purpose.*

It is no wonder therefore that with a strong teleological system at the heart of every living cell, evolution can proceed along its blind path, guided only by natural selection, and at the same time produce creatures who show every appearance of being ruled by purpose. And that appearance becomes closer and closer to reality as evolution produces more and more complex organisms, until we arrive at the stage where purpose becomes not merely an appearance but an actual decision to write a book for the purpose of expressing thoughts and ideas for others to read and think about.

We humans are the final proof of biological purpose, and for that we must thank evolution—for which, in turn, we must thank the genetic code and the system that can translate that code from the chemistry of nucleic acids to the chemistry of proteins.

When I first learned biochemistry, I felt a sense of awe. I found it hard to believe that all the magnificent complexity of these biochemical systems arose by lucky accident, or even by evolution. When I came to understand that the translation system was fundamental to the evolutionary process, I realized that the system could not have come about by the same process it is required for. If the translation system itself was a product of evolution, it had to be a very different kind of evolution.

There are theories about how the evolution of the genetic code and the rise of translation from DNA to proteins happened, but none of them are very convincing or explanatory. This is one of the great mysteries of the origin of life (see chapter 7), and I don't know the answer. Whatever it is, I now thank God for the creation that made the biochemistry of life possible.

Given that the evolutionary biochemical mechanism is the ultimate source of biological purpose, and that God has endowed us with a purpose for existence, it is apparent that God's tool to accomplish this was none other than evolution.

Later when I became a theist, I began wondering if the Darwinian paradigm I have described in this chapter was all there was to evolution. I now thought of the fundamental mechanism of the translation system as miraculous, a direct manifestation of God's creative majesty. I also began to wonder if purely accidental random mutations could be the sole source of the variations that allow evolution to make great leaps in biological form and function. I read Stephen Jay Gould, who postulated the theory of punctuated equilibrium from his observations of the fossil record, which showed long periods of little or no change interspersed with brief periods of rapid, major changes in biological features. Examples of these dramatic jumps in a short period include the appearance of vertebrates, mammalian pregnancy, and feathers. But Gould had no notion of how such variations could arise; nor, of course, did I.

I have many friends who grew up in a Christian household where evolution was considered an atheistic idea. With time and education, many of these friends began to see that the science of evolutionary biology was convincing. Some of them then decided to abandon Christianity completely, since they felt that if the faith was wrong about the interpretation of Genesis, it must be wrong about everything. This, sadly, is an all-too-common scenario. Most of them, however, studied more and began to understand that acceptance of evolution need not entail giving up one's faith in God or the message of Christ. But in order to see this, we must reject the recent interpretation (which some have called heretical) that treats the Bible as if it were a science textbook.

My journey, of course, was quite different. I completely accepted the premises of biological evolution long before I even thought of God as being anything other than a fantasy. But as I began to follow my path leading to Christ and as I began reading the Bible with attention, I also struggled with the idea of reconciling my newfound interest in biblical truth with what I already knew to be true about evolution. Eventually I came to accept a theological worldview that has been called theistic evolution, or evolutionary creationism (discussed in chapter 12). Many of my friends in the Christian community arrived at the same place coming from the other direction.

We can only stand in awe of the magnificent, divine handiwork of evolutionary action in the making of life's diversity.

In chapter 12 we will find some answers to the questions posed here. As we will see, there are constraints on what life can do. We are learning more and more about those constraints and finding some of the basic laws that life must follow. But within that very broad framework, there is so much possibility, so many avenues of progress, that we can only stand in awe of the magnificent, divine handiwork of evolutionary action in the making of life's diversity.

CHAPTER 6

People

ARE HUMAN BEINGS *special, and, if so, how did we get that way?*

I have met folks who more or less accept evolution when it comes to plants and animals, but they draw the line at people. I can understand that, and in a way I even agree with it. Not in the sense that I doubt the common descent of all living things on this planet—what I mean is that I strongly believe that people are special. But are they?

There is a widely held view these days that humans are not very special at all. This popular attitude, which I call "anti-humanism," began after the cultural revolution of the 1960s. It is now easy to find television specials, magazine articles, and endless posts on the internet about how tiny our planet is, how insignificant we are as a species, and how we love to fool ourselves with our imagined self-importance. The evolutionary theorist Stephen Jay Gould said that humans are a minor sideshow, and the true rulers of the earth are bacteria. According to some adherents of modern anti-humanism, people are not a blessing but a curse, and I have heard it said with all seriousness that it would be "better" (I am never quite sure *for whom* it would be "better") if we just disappeared and allowed nature to reclaim the planet.

I have always believed that human beings are exceptional, even miraculous, creatures. When I was growing up, this idea was common among atheists (though they would not have been caught using any form of the word *miracle*, of course). The original secular humanists (including myself) held this view. I believed that evolution had produced a truly remarkable and unique biological entity that had powers never before found in nature. I also thought that human evolution is just in its infancy, and that humanity represents a new and positive force in the universe that could be equivalent in importance and power to the forces released after the big bang. I was brought up to believe that humanism was an important part of being an atheist: the transcendental exceptionalism of humankind was far better, after all, than the concept of a superior God, not to mention what was then my understanding of the Christian doctrines of original sin and the inherent evil of all humans.

In an ironic twist of fate, some modern atheists and agnostics seem to have begun to subscribe, at least in part, to the new antihumanism. Carl Sagan and Neil deGrasse Tyson in their respective *Cosmos* TV series liked to stress the vastness of the universe and the insignificance of our place in it (as if being on a small planet far from the center of a galaxy meant anything in terms of our value and importance). Many people are positive that the universe is full of civilizations more advanced than we are. Jerry Coyne, the archetype of the new militant atheism, has written: "I'm not sure whether the question 'What does it mean to be a human?' has an answer more meaningful than the question 'What does it mean to be a wombat?' Even *asking* that question about our species tends to conjure up some notion of human exceptionalism, sometimes verging on the numinous."[1]

One wonders whether a wombat philosopher warning fellow wombats about the complacency of wombat exceptionalism would use humans, koalas, or kangaroos as her "foil" species.

I do not think that anti-humanism has become an integral part of the new atheist credo—there are certainly exceptions to the trend. But the theme of worthless, polluting, selfish human beings ruining the planet while soothing themselves with their belief in a mythical sky daddy is widespread on the internet, especially on websites frequented by younger and not completely educated followers of the new atheist movement.

Since I had been "pro-human" from my youth, finding out that human beings indeed have a special place in the cosmos was not part of my faith journey. I had always known that, and by the time I became aware of the anti-humanism of some of the new atheist leaders, I had long given up my atheism. But if I had not, I would probably have been badly shaken that my fellow enlightened thinkers abandoned the concept of human exceptionalism. Even now, I sometimes find that to be more disturbing than loss of faith in a deity.

Which Other Animal?

Maybe it is just that I really like human beings. They can smile in a way that bacteria never seem to rival. I have seen poetry that elevates the writer to a level far above that of other species. And while not all rhyming lines scribbled on Valentine's cards are at the level of William Butler Yeats, I cannot think of another animal that can write even bad poetry. Which other animal argues eloquently by striking keys on a small machine that turn up as meaningful symbols on bright screens and are then read by others living thousands of miles away? Which other animal could have invented all the things necessary for all that to happen: language, writing, computers, the internet, wireless connections, and so on?

Which other animal could come up with the idea of exploring the world they live in using experiments and observations, mathematics and argument, and endless discussions? Which other animal has had a new idea or would devote its life to the pursuit of knowledge or the contemplation of mystery or the betterment of the world? Which other animal even *cares* about the world? Or understands that there *is* a world?

Which other animal feels joy at the sound of Bach or the sight of Kandinsky? Which one can do what Bach and Kandinsky did? Which other animal has changed the world so much? Which other animal has managed to fly around the world without wings, to make so much stuff, to have such pleasure through all of its senses, to feel joy and sorrow for the sake of others of their own species? Which other animal has any regard at all for any other species?

No, we are not just another animal. That is so obvious to me that I find it difficult to express it. We are not just special and unique. We are quite wonderful. Let me tell you a story—a mundane and yet amazing story.

An Ordinary Human Takes an Ordinary Trip

One day, I was driving from New York toward Washington, DC, listening to a book on tape by English crime novelist P. D. James. As I drove past the toll barrier at the Delaware Memorial Bridge, I suddenly had a thought of surprising force, such that I became too distracted to continue listening to the tape. It dawned on me that I had just driven a very large, heavy machine at about eighty miles an hour (only a bit over the speed limit) over a large and elaborate bridge, and had then gone through the toll barrier without stopping because my E-ZPass device had sent a signal to the scanner, which allowed the toll to be automatically deducted from my bank account. And while I was doing this, I was listening to a British actress of amazing talent perform a reading of an elaborate and detailed mystery plot, using several voices and accents for the various characters in the story. The power of the reading and of the original writing had transported my consciousness from New Jersey to the Dorset countryside, so beautifully described by Lady James, and immersed me in the subtle and intricate nuances of English culture, so different from my own.

And my thought was: how stunning is all this.

No primate before the last hundred years or so had ever moved at speeds anywhere near to how fast I was traveling, and yet, somehow, I had no difficulty or fear of doing so. How could that be? Why are humans able to move at such speeds without freezing in sheer terror? And look at what people have made: a lovely car, with a complex engine, running on a fuel that is pumped from the ground. What would our ancestors think of an automobile? And that whole E-ZPass thing. What would my grandfather think of that? What incredible technology we have. And what talent! That actress, who brings the written words of a brilliant writer to life with her voice. And then, of course, the writer. The one who thinks of the story. Where did she get the ideas? Every sentence is another idea. How does she do that? And how can my mind deal with all of this so easily?[2]

> ## We are used to miracles, and we call them human nature.

There is, of course, nothing at all unusual about a man driving on a highway listening to an audiobook. But that's only because we are thinking in terms of *our* world, the human world. I would submit that the twenty or thirty phenomena that are included in that simple scenario are, in any sort of natural world, miraculous. The fact that we don't see them as such means simply that we are used to miracles, and we call them human nature.

This is not to argue that our natures are not a result of natural selection, at least to some extent. But I think that anyone who concludes that human genius and human talent (the talent of the writer, of the actor, of the engineers who designed the car, the bridge, and the software, my own ability as a driver, and so on) are totally explained by a few hundred years of natural selection has a very hard case to make.

I know that I am a primate. A hominid, to be precise. I need food and water. I crave a mate and shelter. I like security and I am wary of danger. I also am very aware of my evil side, and even more so of the evil history of my fellow beings. We hominids are selfish and greedy; we can be violent and defensive. We can be uncaring about others and the environment in which we live.

And yet, still as a hominid, I find myself not staring out at the rain from my cave, wondering when I will eat next, but driving a large machine at high speed, listening to a woman from another culture act out a story written by another woman. And then a third woman interrupts all this. My Bluetooth device chirps, and I talk to my love, who is calling me from her cell phone hundreds of miles away. I find this to be a wonderful thing, this being human. And I am very thankful.

Yes, we are primates, but somehow we must account for the masterpieces of art, astounding works of literature, mathematics, self-sacrifice, leadership, poetry, internet chat forums, the composition of a sublime symphony by a deaf composer, the articulation of the physics of singularities by a paralyzed scientist, the daily endurance and love of "ordinary" people.

Why do we paint? Why do we make up stuff and write it down? What good is music? And why do I sit down and type on a keyboard to communicate things to be read by people I have never met? I think it's the same reason we ask, "How does that work?" "Why does this happen?" or "What is behind that thing I see?" Science, music, art, philosophy, love, and humor are not necessary for existence—we could live without them. But they are all part of what it means to be human. So why are we the way we are?

I know I haven't really answered the question. Not convincingly, not by just painting a vignette. That is definitely not scientific!

But here's what I believe. I believe that the existence of modern human beings derives from two different sources. The process of evolution by natural selection produced our bodies, including our brains and minds. In what follows, I will describe some of what is known about how we got here through evolution. But I maintain that our physical nature is not all that defines us, and evolution cannot account for everything that makes us human. The rest of the story of the origin of humanity will be told in the next chapter.

The Evolution of Humans

There is overwhelming scientific evidence that humanity is a part of the evolutionary tree that includes all of life. Sixty million years ago, the earth was full of animals and plants. There were flowers, insects, birds, fish, and small mammals. The process of evolution by natural selection had been going on for over three billion years. There had been at least five major extinctions, each followed by new waves of evolution. With the disappearance of the dinosaurs, the smaller, weaker mammals had a chance to diversify and take over the planet, and they did. Horses, hippos, elephants, bears, wolves, cats—a rich panoply of mammals appeared. Many of them went extinct as well. Among the types of animals that blossomed and prospered after the dinosaur extinction were the primates.

By five million years ago, there were primates of many types around the world. Lemurs, monkeys, and apes (gorillas, orangutans, gibbons) had been evolving for millions of years. Among these primates was a rare group of animals who stood upright on two legs: the hominins. We don't know how many species of hominins there were, not only because we haven't found the remains of all of them, but also because we're not always certain how the ones we've found were related to each other, and which ones were different species. But we do know they have been around for a long time: some (such as *Ardipithecus kadabba*) have been dated as more than five million years old.

These were pretty smart animals. They were not monkeys or apes, though they shared a common ancestor with their primate cousins. The older hominins—*Ardipithecus* and *Australopithecus*—resembled chimpanzees more than they resembled us: they were more animals than human. They had brains about the size of other primates, or only slightly larger, and they lived mostly in trees. But the fact that they walked upright gave them some advantages: they had free hands with which they could hold and carry things—and even make things. The creatures at the beginning of the film *2001: A Space Odyssey* were probably meant to be some form of *Australopithecus*.

About two million years ago, new forms of hominins evolved from a branch of *Australopithecus*. We call this genus *Homo*. The earliest species, *Homo habilis*, goes back two million years; others are much more recent.

There haven't been enough fossils found to fill in all the details of the million or more years of evolution of our genus, but based on anthropological and archeological evidence, we believe that two hundred thousand years ago, there were at least three species of *Homo* around. *Homo neanderthalensis* lived in Europe and parts of western Asia between four hundred thousand and forty thousand years ago. They had large brains—even larger than ours—and they were quite smart. Neanderthals might have been able to talk, but they probably didn't have complex language. They used fire and made sharp stone tools—knives and axes—as well as wooden clubs and spears. They hunted and used animal skins as clothing. Some anthropologists think of them as very similar to us, and there is evidence for limited interbreeding with our own ancestors. But they were not us. In Asia there was an even older species called *Homo erectus*, as well as the Denisovans (who also seem to have contributed genes to some modern human populations through interbreeding). These are species we know less about, except that they also weren't like us. The most recent *Homo* species evolved in Africa about three hundred thousand years ago and quickly replaced all the other hominins living there. These are the *Homo sapiens*, and they are special because they are us.

What made the genus *Homo* unique was their brains. They not only walked upright, but their brains were getting larger, and they were making more and more sophisticated tools. During a period of over a million years, the brain size and intelligence of *Homo* species kept increasing, from around six hundred cubic centimeters in *Homo habilis* to around fourteen hundred cubic centimeters in *Homo sapiens*. This was presumably due to the advantage intelligence affords for survival for animals that are not very fast and have no sharp teeth or claws. Smart animals are more successful than dumb ones, all else being equal. However, despite being smart, the genus *Homo* turned out to be among the least successful of all animals that have evolved on the planet. All species of this genus have gone extinct except one. Neanderthals only survived a few hundred thousand years. Their populations were small and fairly limited geographically.

We *Homo sapiens* also barely managed to survive, with population numbers often falling to near unsustainable levels. Our big brains allowed for increased social interaction and creativity in defending against predators and hunting and gathering food, but they were also a burden. Brains use a huge amount of energy, which can be provided by eating meat, difficult for a primate with weak teeth. In addition, large brains meant large heads, which made reproduction more difficult. Human childbirth became increasingly dangerous, and human children were helpless and needed intensive care for longer periods than any other animal.

Every person alive today is part of this one African species—*Homo sapiens*. We know from genetic studies that all human beings are closely related. Data from population genetics has shown that there is less genetic variation between any two humans (say a South African Sān and a Norwegian) than there is between two chimps in a single group.[3]

How could this be? One possible answer is that at some time between fifty thousand and seventy-five thousand years ago, our species was on the brink of extinction, probably due to a sudden cooling and drying of the climate after the eruption of a supervolcano.[4] This idea (called the Toba catastrophe theory) is controversial, but there are genetic results suggesting that the entire human population decreased to as few as two to ten thousand individuals, putting us on the endangered species list for sure. There may in fact have been several such population "bottlenecks" leading to all of us descending from a very small group of ancestors with very similar genetics.

Around the same time—perhaps in response to challenges posed by the climate, or perhaps due a genetic mutation that spread quickly through the population—there was a very noticeable change in how people lived. Scientist and civilization scholar Jared Diamond calls this phenomenon the "great leap forward" and describes it in great detail in his influential book *The Third Chimpanzee*.[5] This phenomenon is also known as the Upper Paleolithic revolution, or simply behavioral modernity.

During this period, humans started using new materials: bone, shells, antlers, and ivory were added to stone and wood tools for hunting and domestic use. In addition, the technology became more sophisticated and specialized. True blades (sharp tools that are at least twice as long as they are wide and have parallel sides) became the norm, and composite tools appeared. In other words, knives started to look like knives, and there were different kinds of knives—long, short, big, small—clearly made for different purposes.

People became more and more inventive. They figured out how to catch fish using hooks, nets, and fishing spears. They made needles and began sewing clothes that fit better and provided more warmth than an animal skin simply thrown over the body. Bows and arrows made their first appearance, as did vessels for carrying food and water.

There is evidence that people began transporting materials long distances from where they were found (such as rock or flint quarries), suggesting the origin of commerce and trade. Jewelry, as well as painting, sculpture, and decorative arts, appeared for the first time. Burial rituals indicate the possible beginning of religious behavior. There is indirect evidence that language became the kind of language we know, capable of expressing emotions and thoughts using a complex grammatical structure and broad and subtle symbolism. It is likely that music, humor, and romantic love arrived on the scene as well. In other words, everything that makes us human, everything that distinguishes us from the other animals, apparently appeared during this period.

With all these advances, human beings began to prosper. Within a few thousand years, there was a tremendous increase in the population. Finding food became easier, and protection from predators and the cold allowed many who would otherwise have died to survive. A new type of creature roamed the earth, a creature who became prey for no other and predator to all.

The human species began to travel and settle the world. Small numbers of people left Africa and moved into the Middle East and Europe, displacing the Neanderthals. They settled every corner of the globe with great success, including Australia and the Americas.

Recently, the concept of the Upper Paleolithic revolution has come under fire. Many anthropologists hold that there was no revolution—no sudden and rapid change—at all, and behavioral modernity evolved gradually, along with anatomical modernity. But whether sudden or gradual, the change happened, and what emerged roughly forty to fifty thousand years ago was us: fully modern human beings with all the abilities, faults, and desires that we now have.

This is one part of the story of human origins—one that raises more questions than it answers. We have a good idea of what happened in human evolution, but we have not yet looked at how or why it happened. And we have said very little about the origins of those aspects of *Homo sapiens* that make us what we define as human. We will look more closely at those questions in the next chapter.

The following fable looks at how God might think about human exceptionalism. We can imagine this scene taking place around the time of the Upper Paleolithic revolution. It includes a few thoughts and speculations (not all of which I really believe are true).

A Fable About Human Exceptionalism

God was getting reports on how things were going in the universe. As usual, He was especially interested in life. After hearing from a host of angels about life on 8,456,892 planets in the universe, Archangel Gabriel mentioned Earth.

"Lord, evolution has been proceeding quite well on Earth. There have been some very good results with animals. The following have acquired the requisite skills:

Intelligence—crows, dolphins, humans, dogs, whales;

Musical ability—birds, whales, humans;

Communication—many of them, but especially bees, whales, apes, humans, ants, birds;

Use of tools—birds, humans, chimps;

Humor—humans, chimps, dogs . . ."

"The birds sound promising—are those the flying ones?" God interjected.

Gabe confirmed this and reminded God that they were the survivors of those wiped out by God's most recent extinction experiment on the planet.

And then God asked the key question: "Do they worship Me?"

Gabe looked a bit nonplussed. "Um, not as far as we can tell, Lord. At least not yet. It looks like only one kind actually knows and worships You, Lord. The humans."

"Really?" said the Lord. "There isn't much special about them, is there?"

Gabe looked down at the list and nodded. "That's right, Lord. But we have lots of good information on their worship. They praise You, pray to You, and seek Your guidance and support."

"And the dolphins or the bees don't do that? Not even the crows?"

"Apparently not, Lord."

The Lord God thought about this for a while. Then He spoke: "Gabriel, how well do your field agents know this planet?"

"Well, Lord, the closest one is on Bragaphon, which is in a nearby galaxy, Alpha Centauri."

"Hmm. I think we might need an actual site visit. Send somebody there. I want to make sure that the other promising kinds, like the crows, really aren't worshipping Me. I think we need better data."

Gabriel agreed, but then he decided not to send anyone. He needed a break from all the office work and resolved to go himself. He knew that God favored the birds (or any creature that knew how to fly), but Gabriel himself was curious about the humans. True, they were only one of many who were intelligent, used tools and humor, and could communicate and make music, but maybe, just maybe, they were better at all these things than all the other kinds. Maybe even a lot better. And they really did seem to be aware of their Creator. He would go and find out.

When Gabriel returned to heaven, he made an appointment to speak with God. And from the moment Gabriel made his report, everything in the universe changed forever. God was delighted. He had been seeking a good place for His Son to be born, and now He had found it. Everything was perfect. Well, almost.

"Too bad they can't fly," He murmured to Gabriel.

Gabe smiled. "Give them time, Lord. Who knows?"

Of course, I wrote this fable to express my own ideas about humankind—and, as a result, I end up unfortunately implying that God chose us because we showed signs of being exceptional. I should make it clear that that is not what I actually believe, at least not now. I might have thought something along those lines before I understood the basics of Christianity, back when I believed in human exceptionalism but had no idea why it was true. Now I believe that God made us the way we are, as attested to in Genesis when Adam is given the task of naming all the creatures. No other animal can name anything (unless we teach them), and language is one of those key human features that is a gift from God.

While I have always believed that humans are special, I never knew why or how that happened. I was never convinced by the purely evolutionary idea that somehow our brains jumped several orders of magnitude in power and complexity and within less than a hundred thousand years produced us. It was a mystery to me. But when I began to think that God might be real, that perhaps what the Bible says about the origin of humankind could be a real clue to what happened, the mystery began to seem solvable.

And so it wasn't just the two great mysteries of the origin of the universe and the origin of life that had me wondering. To them I added the origin of humanity as we are today, and I pondered what it was that made these three origins so challenging and interesting.

CHAPTER 7

Origins

How did the universe, life, and human consciousness arise?

There are three major origins in our world that have been difficult to explain or even to study scientifically. These are:

The origin of the universe (space, matter, energy, and time)
The origin of life
The origin of human consciousness

These three origins loom as large gaps in our scientific understanding. It would be a God-of-the-gaps fallacy to presume that because the three origins are currently not well understood, no good scientifically describable explanations for them could exist.

But even assuming that we do eventually come to a better understanding of how these three most important existences began, we are still left with a big question: *Why* is it so difficult to understand the origins of the universe, life, and human consciousness today? Scientists have been able to answer a great number of questions about many aspects of how our world works. So why does the naturalistic, scientific approach have so much trouble explaining origins?

This question first dawned on me during the period that I was slowly considering the possibility of God's existence. I wondered what there was about origins that made this kind of question intractable to human understanding. I could find no ready answer to this, and I began to see that the concept of God as Creator, as the source of all origins, was something that made sense. Once I could get past the obstacles preventing me from believing in a supernatural God, I could see that a divine creation was a coherent and logical concept. Now, as a theist, I believe that if and when we do finally gain some scientific understanding of the origin of the universe, the origin of life, and the origin of human consciousness, we will find further pointers to the creative action of God.

> My contemplation of all three origins
> played a major role in opening my mind
> to the reality of a creative divinity.

My contemplation of all three origins played a major role in opening my mind to the reality of a creative divinity. When I first learned the fact that the universe had an origin, a beginning, it was as surprising and disturbing to me as it had been to many other atheist and agnostic scientists, including Fred Hoyle, who coined "big bang" as a term of derision. I had no idea what to make of the obvious connection between the beginning of the Bible and the big bang theory. Later, as a professional biochemist interested in evolution as well as the mechanisms of life, I dove deeply into the origin of life and found . . . a blank mystery. In the previous chapter, I described my long-lasting conviction (predating my conversion to faith) that human beings are exceptional creatures. But the looming question remained: How did we get that way? Let's take a look at each of the origins in more detail, in the order of their appearance.

The Origin of the Universe

The dominant scientific worldview at the end of the nineteenth century was that the universe had no beginning and no end. Ever since the Copernican revolution, as awareness of the heliocentric model of the solar system spread, the general understanding had been that the universe is stable and static—that it has always existed as it is now, and always would. This was considered the rational, naturalistic view when Einstein worked on relativity and gravity about a hundred years ago. The notion of a static universe was of course irreconcilable with the biblical account of a creation by God: scientists scoffed at that story. If God created the universe, they would ask, then what was there before? And who created God, and when exactly did this God decide to create the universe? And where did He get all that matter and energy?

But as irrational and weird as a beginning of the universe might have seemed to nineteenth-century scientists, it turned out to be true. We now have strong evidence that the universe was not always here, that it had a beginning, and that before that beginning there was no matter, no energy, and no time—therefore, there actually was no *before* in any sense we can discuss. The big bang was a singularity, something outside of the laws of physics, which themselves developed during the first 10^{-40} seconds after the big bang.

When Einstein found that some implications of his general theory of relativity would result in a non-static, collapsing universe, he added a "cosmological constant" to cancel out the attractive force of gravity. Einstein later said this was an error. However, in an amazing twist (not that unusual in science), it seems, based on the discovery of the inflationary accelerated expansion of the universe, that Einstein was actually correct, and the cosmological constant is now back.

In the 1920s, spectroscopic observations found that the light from many distant galaxies displayed a redshift—a lengthening of the wavelength toward the red end of the spectrum. (This is a form of the Doppler effect, the same phenomenon that causes us to hear a train whistle change its pitch as it passes us.) The finding suggested that these galaxies are moving away from us. Edwin Hubble (working from the data of Henrietta Swan Leavitt and Vesto Slipher) found that all galaxies are moving away from each other everywhere in the universe. He and other astronomers proposed, based on these observations, that the entire universe is expanding. Georges Lemaître (a Belgian priest and physicist) went further and suggested that if it were true that the universe was expanding continuously and everywhere, then at some point in time, all the matter and energy in the universe must have been in one spot, until with an enormous explosion everything began to expand (and is still expanding). That explosion could be timed to about thirteen billion years ago. The later discovery of cosmic background radiation gave further confirmation to this theory, and alternative theories of a steady-state universe with no beginning, favored by Hoyle and others, were dropped. The idea that there was a single moment of creation is currently established science.

A number of physicists initially rejected the idea of the big bang because it seemed too close to the origin theory presented in the Bible. It seemed to represent a victory for creationism, and many atheists did not like that idea at all. After all, if science is truth and religion is falsehood, then what can atheists say when science itself seems to favor the "falsehoods" of religion? Awkward indeed!

The sudden creation from nothing (ex nihilo) of matter, energy, and time is hard to explain as anything other than a miracle. Calling it a "singularity" sounds very scientific, but it is really just another word for a miracle: a mystery undetermined by the laws of our universe and thus inaccessible to scientific investigation. When

Christians say God is outside of time and space, some atheists will argue that this is impossible or meaningless. And yet, if the only alternative to God (based on the fine-tuning argument discussed in chapter 3) is a multiverse, it makes no sense to say that God cannot exist outside of space and time, because something has to: either other universes or God.

The big bang was not only the start of the universe but also the beginning of time. It makes no sense to ask how long it took for the big bang to happen. That concept is very hard to grasp, since our brains find it hard to imagine that as we go back in time, there's a point where the word *before* has no meaning.

Our universe is far from equilibrium. It had a beginning (the big bang), and it is likely to have an end. In a dynamic universe such as ours, time is an important component: the key processes of the universe, including increasing entropy (disorder) and decreasing temperature, are functions of time. All the events that have occurred and are occurring, from galaxy formation to supernovas, occur in time and follow the laws and forces expected in a dynamic, cooling, quantum-based (particle-based) universe.

Learning about cosmological fine-tuning (chapter 3) and the big bang had a profound effect on my worldview. I did understand that a fine-tuning argument for God had a God-of-the-gaps problem— at some point, some genius might find a theory that shows that all the cosmological constants must be exactly what they are based on a new law of physics or even on a new interpretation of existing laws. But I also understood that the multiverse idea raises the same questions that the God idea does—where did the multiverse come from? What created that?

My rational mind began to wonder about the possibility that the God hypothesis might not be excluded by science—and may even be supported by it.

One question that remained was this: After the universe was

created thirteen billion years ago, was everything that later happened preordained, or were there further creation events? I could not fathom how the laws of nature that governed the universe from the time of the big bang would have possibly allowed for the emergence of life. I now believe that the origin of life was the second major creation event, and I have found no science to contradict that belief.

The Origin of Life

The question of how life began is extremely difficult to answer using science. To understand abiogenesis (the origin of life from nonlife) is to understand a long process that led from a world of chemicals to the last universal common ancestor (the ancestor of all life on earth today), which was a living cell encased in a membrane, complete with DNA, many proteins, a genetic code, metabolic machinery, and energy conversion reactions.

The idea that a modern type of cell—containing DNA, RNA, proteins and all the machinery to allow for metabolism, replication of DNA, and translation of a genetic code to produce a specific phenotype—could arise by spontaneous generation is not scientifically tenable and is rejected by scientific consensus. Instead, it is universally assumed that the origin of life must have been a stepwise process and that the earliest living cells must have been quite different from anything alive today.

"How did life begin?" is not really one question but a long series of questions. At the early part of the change from chemistry to biology, we need to ask questions about how the building blocks of life—the amino acids, nucleotides, and lipids—were formed and arose in sufficient concentration to be assembled into the polymers that are a requirement for life. Then the next question is: Once the building blocks were there, how did such an assembly take place? Were conditions on the very early earth appropriate for the required chemical reactions? What were the first catalysts, in the absence of proteins, to allow synthetic reactions to take place at the velocity necessary for life or proto-life?

Other questions follow. What energy sources could have been used to fuel the chemical reactions? How did photosynthesis arise? Where did a genetic code come from? How did the translation machinery develop? Did all of these mechanisms arise stepwise? These questions contain within them many more questions, each of them the subject of research investigations.

There are a number of scientific theories for the origin of life, but currently no theory is complete or more convincing than the others. There are so many questions and problems, and so few good experimental approaches to answer them, that speculation is the rule. Physicists have presented theories about energy dissipation and offered logical approaches to the subject of complexity. Chemists chime in with the propensities of clays and minerals to act as catalysts. There are discussions of hypercycles of metabolic reactions, spontaneous formation of membranes, growth of polymers, abiotic synthesis of amino acids and nucleotides, and organic compounds arriving on meteors.

Traditionally, the scientific field of origin-of-life research has been divided into two camps based on what theorists propose came first: replication or metabolism. The replicators-first group think that once molecules (like DNA or RNA) capable of self-replication appeared, metabolism was sure to follow. The other group counters that even with a base-pairing mechanism in place, replication is not possible without enzymes and metabolic processes in place first (see chapter 4).

Both sides are probably right: it's the classic chicken-or-egg problem. Without enzymes and metabolism, it's hard to imagine efficient and accurate replication. But without replication, any advanced metabolism that arises in a particular proto-cell cannot survive into the next generation. I started out as a firm believer in the replicator-first idea, since I worked in genetics and loved everything about DNA. More recently, I was persuaded that metabolism first makes a stronger case. But of course, what I believe now is that life could not have gotten started without divine help.

The most widely held scientific theory for any part of abiogenesis is that an "RNA world" of life arose first and then morphed into the modern DNA world. The idea came from the finding that some RNA molecules (like the ribosome) can act as pretty good catalysts called ribozymes. It is possible that at some early point in the history of life, cells could have contained sufficiently long RNA molecules to act as both catalysts (enabling metabolism) and as replicators (with the capacity for genetic information storage). RNA provided the required tight linkage between genotype and phenotype, since both genotype and phenotype are part of the same RNA molecule. Furthermore, there is evidence that modern ribozymes, like the ribosome, may exist in modern cells as "molecular fossils" of those very early life-forms. Some researchers have shown that populations of RNA ribozymes can even evolve in the laboratory.

While an RNA world has been the most popular intermediate hypothesis for early life, there are still no good ideas about how such a world could have started or how it could have transformed into our modern DNA world. While most scientists in the field regard an RNA world as a plausible hypothesis, others have raised some problems regarding its likelihood. These problems include the chemical difficulty of spontaneous emergence of RNA molecules that were long enough for replicase activity and a lack of clarity on how many different RNA molecules in a single cell would allow for any sort of natural selection. It is clear that something must have come before an RNA world, but that earlier world remains a mystery.

Despite these problems, let's for the moment assume that RNA-based life-forms arose somehow and achieved some degree of success as living cells. In order to explain the life we know today, at some point there must have been a shift to DNA-based life. The advantages of the modern DNA-based life system include the possibility of much greater complexity, providing a far more efficient process of natural selection. This is because such a system allows the production of an enormous array of proteins, most of them catalytic enzymes, which in turn can assume an astonishing variety of structural and functional roles.

For our DNA world to work, there must be a genetic code that allows for the translation of the order of bases in DNA into the correct structure of the cellular proteins. The genetic code is the first instance of pure symbolic information in the universe that we know about.

So how did something as novel as the symbolic information of the genetic code arise? There are some theories, but little evidence. The proponents of intelligent design claim that any spontaneous, naturalistic explanation for the origin of the genetic code is simply impossible. The problem with that approach is that even assuming that God is the Author of the code and of life (which I do assume), there may still be a discoverable natural mechanism by which God acted to create. All of nature is created by God, including everything for which we have found natural mechanisms.

In any case, the genetic code is far more than an interesting chemical novelty. Eugene Koonin, a leader in the field of abiogenesis research (who is not a theist), has acknowledged the difficulty: "The translation system might appear to be the epitome of irreducible complexity because, although some elaborations of this machinery could be readily explainable by incremental evolution, the emergence of the basic principle of translation is not. Indeed, we are unaware of translation being possible without the involvement of ribosomes, the complete sets of tRNA and aminoacyl-tRNA synthetases (aaRS), and (at least, for translation to occur at a reasonable rate and accuracy) several translation factors. In other words, staggering complexity is inherent even in the minimally functional translation system."[1]

If the modern translation system with a genetic code nevertheless did evolve gradually (like all other biological systems), then it must have started out much simpler and much more susceptible to errors. One problem is that unless this system is almost error-free, no evolution is possible. Below a certain threshold of accuracy, genetic improvements in the function of the proteins, RNA, and cofactor molecules that are part of the system will not be handed down, and thus no selection will take place.

Time presents another problem for abiogenesis. It was once thought that life appeared several billion years after the formation of the earth. That made sense, since in the absence of natural selection, the genesis of life would have required many highly improbable reactions to all occur at the same time. But with every year, it seems that the origin of life gets pushed further back, closer to the beginning of earth's history—leaving less time for abiogenesis to occur. It now appears that as far back as four billion years ago, life-forms used most of the same basic principles and materials that all living creatures use today. This is only a few hundred million years after the planet cooled! It is astonishing that in such a brief time span, life was able to form from the simple chemical compounds present on earth, especially when we consider that evolutionary biology indicates it then took about two billion years for the early single-cell life-forms to evolve into multicellular organisms. It doesn't seem to make sense that it would take four to ten times longer for living cells to evolve multicellularity than it did for the first living cell, complete with a DNA-based genetic code, enzymes, and even photosynthesis, to form from simple organic chemicals.

At the end of his awe-inspiring pilgrimage through the evolutionary history of life, *The Ancestor's Tale*, Richard Dawkins states that in his opinion the answer for the origin of life will come in the form of a beautiful and elegant theory because it is such a tough problem that only a major breakthrough, equivalent to the discovery of the double helix or the theory of relativity, will provide an answer. I agree with that. We are still awaiting the insight to come for a natural theory.

> As the laws of physics cannot explain or describe the actual event that triggered the big bang, the laws of biology cannot explain or understand the origin of life.

In analogy with the big bang singularity, I propose that the origin of life was a "biological singularity," since before the origin of life, the laws of biology (in particular, the law of evolution by natural selection) could not operate. The laws that govern biological science were born at the time of the origin of life, along with the first living cell. Just as the laws of physics that emerged at the time of the big bang singularity govern the expansion of the new universe and all subsequent events, so do the laws of biology (including evolution) govern the expansion of life and all subsequent events for living creatures. And as the laws of physics cannot explain or describe the actual event that triggered the big bang, the laws of biology cannot explain or understand the origin of life.

In my own journey toward faith, I began to see that a belief that life began as an act of creation by God is not contradictory to the scientific evidence, and there is no reason for a rational, scientifically oriented individual to avoid such a belief. As soon as one accepts the special creation of the first living cell by God, everything fits into place. The creation of life could then be viewed as the simultaneous creation of a genetic molecule (DNA or RNA) that allows for both self-replication of the genetic molecule and the formation of a code that allows for translation into specific proteins. This makes natural selection possible.

If this special creation is true, then God's creation of life included the process of natural selection as the means to further creation of living forms. If God created life, at the same time He also created the mechanism by which life could evolve. This means that evolution by natural selection is not an argument against the existence of God. Quite the contrary: it stands as a testimony to the creative genius of a divine being who has blessed us not only with stars and matter and energy and all the physical laws of His created universe but also with the plants and animals that have evolved from the operation of the God-given biological law of evolution by natural selection.

Just as we have no idea how biology emerged from chemistry, we also run into a roadblock when we try to understand how the human mind (or soul or consciousness) emerged from biology. This question intrigued me long before I began to believe in anything like the *imago Dei* (image of God). Where did all this creativity of humans come from?

The Origin of Humans

Look around you. Look in the mirror. You are seeing the evidence before your eyes of something miraculous and mysterious. You see a primate, perhaps one who needs a shave or has rings under her eyes from sleepless nights. Perhaps you see an animal who is in misery or pain, who is not eating well, or who is ill. Perhaps this animal in the mirror, or one you pass in the street, is hungry, exhausted, or hurt. But look again. You will see smiles, you will see a sparkle, you will see love. You will hear them sing, laugh, and speak; or cry, worry, and call out for help. You might even see them thinking, writing, inventing, or understanding. You could watch as they pray. These things are a gift from the God who created us and gave us souls. These things are new to the universe, and they make us much more than animals descended from animals; they make us human, closer to the divine. And when God appeared to us in the form of a man, the circle was completed. God created humankind in the image that was needed in order for God Himself to appear on earth.

Or perhaps human beings are simply slightly smarter apes, whose evolutionary history includes some adaptations that give us the illusion of being superior. Consciousness, art, science, music, humor, and conscience are simply part—or neurological manifestations—of this illusion. Human consciousness might just be a convenient delusion, created by natural selection to provide us with some solace to go along with our intelligence. Perhaps humans are indeed merely naked apes, with selfish genomes that are the masters of the universal drive to survive and prosper, and all that we are, all we have done, all of the joy, beauty, love, hope, and sense of right and wrong that define the human condition are without purpose or meaning.

Which view is right? Let's allow science to have a crack at this question.

Human Cultural Evolution

We know that for most plants and animals, the entire phenotype is determined by the genotype. I mean not only the biological characteristics of each individual but also individual and group behavior, like the mating dances of birds, the signaling of bees and ants, the howling of wolves, or the family structures of lions. These behaviors are ultimately of genetic origin, and it requires a genetic change—a change in the genotype—to effect a change in cultural as well as in biological phenotype.

Humankind is the only major exception to this rule. The cultural phenotype of human beings has been changing continuously for about forty thousand years, and the direction of that change has been constant, while the rate of change has been increasing in an exponential manner. At the same time, there have been very few changes in genotype to account for the cultural phenotypic changes.

We are the only species on the planet whose evolution is no longer genetic but cultural, a process driven by our unique brains. The ordinary processes of genetic evolution gave us these brains, but then the brains took over. The physicist George Ellis has described the phenomenon as an example of "top-down" causation, in which higher-level structures (in this case, brains) can affect the same lower-level components (in this case, cells) that produced them, giving rise to new "emergent" properties of complex systems.[2]

The way we live today is completely different from the way human beings lived forty thousand years ago. It is different from the way human beings lived four hundred years ago, and even four years ago. For all other species, this is never true. Chimpanzees today live in the wild very much like they did four million years ago.

A lot has been made of the fact that other animals can solve problems, show altruism, make pictures, communicate, have emotions, have social structures, and do "all" the things that humans do. That is beside the point. What humans do that no other living creature does is change *intentionally*. Humans use their complex brains to overcome biological limitations imposed by a genome that changes very slowly. We, and only we, have the ability to assert our freedom from our genes. Dawkins said in his television documentary *The Genius of Charles Darwin* that "as Darwin recognized, we humans are the first and only species able to escape the brutal force that created us, natural selection. . . . We alone on earth have evolved to the point where we can . . . overthrow the tyranny of natural selection."[3]

It's clear that scientists can agree we are special. Very special. But where did that specialness come from? That is a difficult and controversial question, and one that has resisted a clear answer from science. Christians say that human beings were created in the image of God. Before I came to agree with that view, I thought of the special nature of humans as stemming from something similar to a soul—consciousness.

Human Consciousness

I was always intrigued by the mystery of human consciousness. Until a few decades ago, questions concerning consciousness or the mind were considered outside the realm of science—they were the province of theologians and philosophers only. The entry of scientists (neurobiologists, psychologists, and others) into the study of human consciousness has not led to any real breakthroughs in our understanding of what consciousness is or why we have it. Many answers have been provided, ranging from the denial of the very existence of consciousness to attempts to apply quantum theory or other known laws of physics to the problem. Some have held that the problem of consciousness is not resolvable scientifically.

Philosopher Daniel Dennett exemplifies the first approach: he maintains that human consciousness of the higher type, the sense of awareness we all have of being ourselves, the experience of the "essence" of who we are, is not actually real but an illusion created by our brain physiology shaped by natural selection.[4] He is in the minority, though—there is a consensus of sorts that holds that intelligence is a survival trait and might be explained by natural selection, but consciousness is not. For one thing, no one has been able to explain how being conscious could provide a selective advantage. If anything, it might be just the opposite.

Attempts at describing what it means to be conscious have not been very helpful in understanding where consciousness comes from, beyond identifying it as being a property of certain animal brains. The complexities of the neural process in humans explain the senses, thoughts, memories, and a good deal of creativity and imagination. But studies of neural connections, pathways, interactions, and anatomies have not really answered the basic question: How does consciousness arise? I think it's unlikely that pure neurology will answer this. I am sure we will find more brain regions that are "responsible" for spiritual, religious, artistic, or ethical thoughts and ideas, but that doesn't get us closer to the answer. We still don't know what any of those things are, just as we ultimately cannot define consciousness.

Whether we answer the question of the origin of human consciousness in terms of God or in terms of a naturalistic explanation involving an emergent quality of our incredibly complex brains, the fact remains that human beings exhibit behaviors not explainable by natural selection.

Before I found God, while I was searching for an understanding of human nature, I liked the idea that consciousness might be something that emerges from the concentrated complexity of neural interactions in human brains. I thought of consciousness as an emergent phenomenon of complex life that cannot be entirely explained by the laws of biology—in the same way that life is an emergent phenomenon of complex chemistry, but it cannot be entirely described or explained by the laws of chemistry.

And that was as far as I could get, until I took the next step in my journey toward faith. I knew that humans were special, but I could not explain how that happened or what it meant. I had no belief in *imago Dei* or a soul. I was still looking to science for all my answers. I needed to discover that science has limits, and that there are some questions it cannot answer.

CHAPTER 8

The Limits of Science

How do we go beyond the limits to the scientific approach to under-standing and knowledge?

Several decades ago, I was driving along a country road looking for a cabin owned by a friend of mine. The directions he had given me were vague at best. I came to a spot where the very rustic road vanished completely. To confirm that I had reached the end of the road, there was an old sign that read: STOP! NO MOTOR VEHICLES BEYOND THIS POINT.

I stopped the car and proceeded to walk a couple of dozen yards along a well-marked footpath to a clearing where I could see the cabin in the distance.

I had been somewhat annoyed when I started walking, since I had a lot of gear in the car that I would need to haul to the cabin, but I got over it, and for the week I stayed there, I came to appreciate the total silence and sense of peace that came with being "off-road."

For many questions about the natural world, we can stay firmly on the road of science as the best or only path to truth; there is no need to go "off-road." What is the chemical composition of DNA?

What are things made of? How do molecules fit together? How does electricity work? Does smoking cause cancer?

When it comes to answering such questions, we have become used to a certain way of moving forward. We have the smooth, well-paved road of science. We travel down that road on our conveyances of rational induction, objective reproducibility, and other vehicles mass-produced by the Rational Materialism Transportation Co. And we almost always get where we want to go, or at least where the road takes us.

But almost always is not always. There are a few roads in our scientific universe that also have stop signs. Signs that say, "Go no further in your vehicle." In order to continue, we need to dismount and go on foot or with some other kind of conveyance.

This is not a popular idea among some modern atheists—those who subscribe to a view philosophers call *scientism* (discussed more later). One definition of scientism could be the belief that such stop signs do not and cannot exist, and that everything we might ever want or need to know about anything can always and only be learned with the scientific method.

As we have seen in chapter 2, modern physics tells us that there are indeed some things we cannot know, and when we arrive at these questions, we encounter stop signs we cannot pass. We know scientifically that the position of an electron cannot be known at the same time as its momentum, ever, anywhere, by anyone. The uncertainty principle exists not because we need to do more research; it's a fact of nature, discovered as the result of research, and it won't change.

Kurt Gödel's first incompleteness theorem is another stop sign related to mathematical certainty. It says, in S. C. Kleene's generally accepted formulation, that "any effectively generated theory capable of expressing elementary arithmetic cannot be both consistent and complete."[1] This means there will always be mathematical statements that are true but are unprovable within the system: uncertainty is a given, inevitable by law. As Johannes Koelman says, "There is no system of logic that is free from contradictions and at the same time free of gaps."[2]

Gödel's theorem has been proven, and it leads to a philosophically interesting conclusion: self-referential models, which include many scientific and mathematical models, can never be absolutely comprehensive and correct. It became clear with Gödel's theorem that not even mathematics (the pure language of science) is immune to uncertainty.

> Scientists have always known that there must be limits to how far we can go in understanding all aspects of reality.

Scientists have always known that there must be limits to how far we can go in understanding all aspects of reality. As we dig deeper into biology, we will come across some stop signs also. There are aspects of cellular biology that are starting to look as impenetrable as quantum mechanics. For example, the regulation of gene expression has a level of complexity that may surpass the ability of science to fully comprehend, making the prediction of outcomes difficult. Of course, a high level of complexity is not the same as a stop sign, and more biological research is still needed before we reach the point where we can go no further using the scientific method.

Models

The stop signs discussed earlier are not the only times we find limits in science. At some point in their education and efforts to explain how the world works, scientists often have a startling revelation that most people never learn about: we can almost never accurately describe the "actual real world" using our scientific tools. That's because everything about the real world is extremely complex, with so many variables that it's almost impossible to take them all into account.

There is a way around this problem that has been used since the dawn of modern science: model building. Sometimes the model is an actual physical object, like the beautiful structure of DNA that James Watson and Francis Crick built in their lab. More often, the model is a formula or equation that makes a number of assumptions that are acknowledged to be not really true. To quote from two chemistry textbooks:

> A model may or may not closely describe a real system; frequently one idealizes or simplifies certain parts . . . in order to render the equations more readily solved. Quite often, if the simplifications are wise, the model systems still give results very close to the behavior of the real systems of interest which are observed in the laboratory.[3]

> In thermodynamics, as in other branches of science, it is convenient to set up model systems to which the behaviour of real systems approximates under limiting conditions. The value of this procedure is that simple and exact relations may be established for the model, to an extent which is impossible for the real systems themselves.[4]

What this means is that a great many of our natural laws are actually descriptions of models of reality rather than of reality itself. For instance, the ideal gas law, which takes the form of an equation of state, is a fundamental bulwark of chemistry. Using this law, if you know the temperature and volume of a gas sample and the number of molecules in it, you can calculate its pressure—or, if you know the volume, pressure, and the number of molecules, you can calculate the temperature, and so on.

And the answer you get will be just right. Well, actually—no, it won't be.

The answer will be *very close* to just right, but you will always be off just a bit. This law is called the *ideal* gas law because it applies to an ideal gas—not the actual gas, but a model of it. An ideal gas has no molecular size (all the molecules are infinitesimal), and there are no forces (like van der Waals forces) between molecules. This is never true for real gases.

The ideal gas law is a good approximation, but it is not an exact description of reality. There are better gas laws that take into account the dimensions of gas molecules and interactive forces, but they are much less elegant, and none are perfect. It turns out that the same thing is true for most of the laws of chemistry and physics, and even more so for biology. This is not a big problem for applications of science, because models usually give answers that are very close to real-world solutions. If they don't, then the models are rejected, and better ones are found. So, while most scientists will agree that using models is perfectly fine, the truth is that in many cases we cannot account for every aspect of the real world, even with our elegant and scientifically derived equations. Of course, as a pilot friend of mine told me, "It's better to be going in *roughly* the right direction than *exactly* the wrong direction!"

The secret about models is not terribly earthshaking in terms of scientific knowledge, but I think acknowledging their limits is important philosophically and theologically. If we want to invoke some form of "purity" of knowledge about the world, we cannot use the scientific method, because that method will give us *good enough* answers but no perfect answers to almost anything. I believe that this truth is telling us something important about the nature of the reality we find ourselves in. It is a reality that lies beyond our ability to *know absolutely*, although we can get very close. At some point in our drive for complete and total knowledge, there will always be a stop sign.

Scientism

Many atheists don't like the term *scientism*. They believe it is absolutely true that only the scientific method can reveal truth and that all truth can be derived by the scientific method, so they find the term derogatory (which it is). But the idea that science can answer all questions is actually a new one; it was never part of the worldview of freethinkers before the rise of militant anti-theism, and it is a throwback to a discredited philosophy called logical positivism.

A few years ago, I heard Ian Hutchinson, a physicist at MIT, give a lecture on this subject at a meeting of the American Association for the Advancement of Science in Washington, DC. Dr. Hutchinson is the author of the book *Monopolizing Knowledge: A Scientist Refutes Religion-Denying, Reason-Destroying Scientism*. The subtitle pretty much tells the story. The lecture was about the rise of scientism, especially within the new atheist community, and about why scientism is wrong—and in fact anti-scientific.

The myth of scientism is now being propagated by a small cabal of militant anti-theists, only a minority of whom are actually working scientists. Even my father, a committed and uncompromising atheist (who was also a chemist), made it quite clear to me that science is only good for answering certain questions and not others. This was the general view at the time I was learning to be a scientist.

One of the best examples of scientism is the overuse and abuse of evolutionary psychology, which is a popular approach to explain consciousness and all the other uniquely human attributes of the human mind and soul by attributing all of them to evolutionary mechanisms. The purpose of this new field is to find "scientific" explanations for human characteristics within the context of evolutionary adaptation. The field is based on the premise that all human behaviors and characteristics are the result of evolutionary adaptations to survival conditions during the evolution of humanity. Sociobiology is a related area of study that also incorporates this premise. Sexual jealousy, hunger for sweets, even altruism toward kin can be explained as evolutionary adaptations, and many of these explanations are reasonable and likely valid. The problem is that overapplying this method leads to cases where the evidence is a mere "just so" story that *sounds* logical and meaningful, but it is not in any way falsifiable. There is no possible human trait, real or imagined, that cannot be postulated to result from some evolutionary selective advantage.

Take, for example, the well-known human tendency to bite one's fingernails when nervous. We could say that long fingernails present an impediment to the manual dexterity needed to properly wield a weapon, and therefore when nervous, the human tends to be sure that his or her fingernails are as short as possible. This is complete nonsense that I just made up without more than a moment's thought, but it sounds good.

Or take a fictional trait, like the urge to urinate when undergoing high-speed movement. That arose because humans never moved at high speeds unless they were being dragged away by a large carnivore, and urination was a useful way to signal distress to any other human passing by and in addition had the potential of disgusting the animal enough to make it let go. Sounds logical.

There is also the question of evolutionary time. Modern humans have been around for fifty to a hundred thousand years and emerged as a biological species about two hundred thousand years before that. These are extremely short time spans for evolution, and it is certainly hard to see how all the human traits we see in thought processes, sexual activities, child-rearing, thinking, language, art, and so on could have evolved so quickly. If, however, these traits evolved in earlier hominin species, we need to be sure that the environment and behavioral selection pressures for those earlier ancestors were equivalent to those of early *Homo sapiens*. This may or may not be true, depending on the situation.

Lurking behind evolutionary psychology is a theological statement that effectively says, "There is no God, and therefore all human characteristics must be explainable by scientific (evolutionary) principles." But if humans are *not* totally explained by evolutionary principles, that leads to the question of what other explanations for human behavior and human nature there could be. There are many answers to this question—some of them theological, others not.

Science and knowledge are not synonymous. In other words, there are other kinds of knowledge that are not scientific—they fall outside of the methods or interests of science. Examples of nonscientific knowledge include history and other "social sciences," art, love, and compassion.

> The denial of any knowledge other
> than the scientific kind gives us
> a distorted view of reality.

Science is marked by two special characteristics—reproducibility and clarity. It is a fundamental hallmark of the scientific method that a result obtained by one person in a given place at a particular time must be obtained by a different person in a different place at a different time to be considered valid. In other words, true knowledge about the natural world should be objective and repeatable. The other characteristic is clarity. Scientific facts and theories must be able to be stated in very clear terms, which is why mathematics is so useful in much of science.

However, scholarship in history and other social sciences is often not repeatable in any way, and history itself does not repeat (though, of course, it can have repeating patterns). Artistic, emotional, and compassionate knowledge does not have clarity—so these types of knowledge cannot be scientific.

Science has become such a powerful tool and has achieved such a high standing in the minds of most people that everyone wants to think of their own discipline as a science. Sociologists can get insulted when told that their field is not science, but the statement does not demean the field of sociology, because other forms of knowledge are just as valuable as science. I once met a professor of English who specialized in fifteenth-century poetry and was a respected scholar in the field. He had a great deal of knowledge about things that most scientists would not even be interested in. But it *was* knowledge. The denial of any knowledge other than the scientific kind gives us a distorted view of reality. By insisting on scientism, we are not only harming nonscientific scholarship; we are also harming science because we are encouraging a misleading understanding of it that can only lead to eventual disillusionment and even the abandonment of science as an activity important for humans.

There are also some scientific ideas that don't quite fit within the normal definition of established science. In some cases, this is because they are still in the formative stage and haven't yet amassed enough (or sometimes any) data to support them. In other cases, the chances of ever getting such data seem remote. Some examples are the natural origin of life and the idea of a multiverse (both discussed in the previous chapter), and the existence of alien civilizations in the universe. These ideas are not wrong, but they are not that far removed from other more spiritual notions of reality, with which they share an absence of evidence. There is not a very bright line between what is called scientific and other forms of knowledge about the reality of the universe. Once we admit that science is not the only valid epistemology, we can open the door to alternative kinds of knowledge, even those that are not objective, repeatable, and clear.

A Constant Mystery

There are many laws in science that are described mathematically. Some are established from experimentation; others are derived theoretically from other known laws. It has often been pointed out that it is quite remarkable that nature operates in ways that can be accurately described by simple mathematical equations.

These equations can be categorized into two classes. Some are purely relational between different measurable and deterministic parameters. The idea that a force exerted by an object is equal to the product of the mass and the acceleration of the object is accurately captured by the simple equation $F = ma$. Each component of the equation is measurable.

The equations in the other category are just as valid, just as true experimentally, but they are less simple in that they require the addition of an entity that is not measurable. These additional components are called constants because they do not change, and they may be determined by experiment or mathematical derivation, but they have no physical reality themselves. In chapter 3, I discussed the fine-tuning of the cosmological constants and their profound importance in making a universe that includes us possible. Here I want to address the *existence* of constants in physical laws because it involves questions we cannot answer scientifically. The very nature of physical constants is confusing. As Venkat Srinivasan writes in an article about unsuccessful attempts to discover variations in the proton-electron mass ratio in the universe, "The weird thing about such constants is that there is no theory to explain their existence. They are universal and they appear to be unchanging."[5]

One of the best-known constants is π from geometry. The area of a circle is determined by its size—namely, its radius or circumference: $A = \pi r^2$.

The value of π is well-known as approximately $3.1415 \ldots$, where the dots indicate that there are an infinite number of decimals. It is called an irrational number because it cannot be expressed as a simple fraction, and thus its exact value can never be known. But where did the value of π come from? Why does it have the value it does, and why is it irrational? We don't know the answers any more than we know why Planck's constant (h), so important in atomic theory and quantum mechanics, is what it is.

One of the most important constants is the speed of light (c). Knowing the value of c allows us to determine many things, including the relationship between mass and energy, as formulated by Einstein: $E = mc^2$. But why does light travel at that speed always, and not faster or slower? That question is not part of science as we understand it.

I believe there is an important philosophical point in the fact that the *reason* the constants have the values they have is *not* subject to scientific inquiry. The existence of fundamental physical constants proves that scientism is wrong. We can of course invoke the emotions one feels when listening to Beethoven, or the source of the creative genius manifested in poetry or painting, to know this. We can defend the concept of love as being more than an evolutionary adaption to reproductive challenges in early hominins. But we can also look at science itself to see its limits quite clearly. We need simply ask why π, h, and c have the values they have—and not accept the common answer that such questions are meaningless and don't matter.

Other *why* questions are clearly deeply important to us, and we don't give up on them easily. That is why there are scientists who consider questions such as "Why is there a universe?" and "Why are people often kind to each other?" to be scientifically approachable. Some of their answers have more scientific rigor and merit than others (see the earlier discussion on evolutionary psychology). But it is clear that when we decide that anything not approachable by science doesn't and cannot exist, we're left with a distorted picture of reality.

We see the same problem with *value* questions. How do we account for what we hold most dear and important to us? Can a poem be *worth* as much to humankind as the result of a scientific experiment? Can there be great truths found in a work of fiction such as *Les Misérables*? I once had an argument with a scientism-believing atheist who disputed my contention that judging the beauty of a work of art was outside of scientific analysis. He argued that I was wrong because the artistic quality of any artwork can be easily quantified by an assessment of its commercial value—the price that would be paid for it. I asked him if he was serious, and he said he was. I had nothing further to say.

So the question is, If and when we come to one of those stop signs that tell us we can go no further in our scientific, rational material-ism vehicles, should we still try to make progress? If we don't want to give up and say, "Well, we go no further with science, so we'll just turn around and go home," then how do we proceed? What kind of vehicle should we find—or should we go on foot? I don't know the answer, but I do know there are a lot of options. We can try the bicycle of philosophy or the skateboard of psychology, or sometimes we might want to use the moped of theology. I would say whatever works is worth a try. Even if it means striking out on foot with whatever crazy, personal, brand-new idea that nobody has ever thought of. We might not get there, but the trip is worth the effort. And who knows what we will find past the stop sign. Once we drop the illusion that the scientific method as we know it is the only and all-powerful path toward understanding truth, we can make a great deal of progress in learning what other truths await our grasp.

In my journey toward faith, I had gone as far as I could in my scientific method automobile. I had reached a number of stop signs in trying to understand the universe using rational logic and science alone. My questions were not being answered, and I could drive no further along the path I was now determined to follow. I had to leave that trusty old car behind and proceed on foot through what seemed to me at the time to be an impenetrable jungle of irrational ideas, superstitions, delusions, and wishful thinking. I stood there under that stop sign for a long time, not knowing what to do, and I would still be there if God had not shown me the way. But He did. The next chapter is about that.

CHAPTER 9

The Call of Faith

UP TO THIS point, I have written about physics, biology, and the important lessons I learned from working in and reading about science. Before we go any further, it might be a good idea to summarize what those lessons were because at this point, my journey, which had been slow and halting for a long time, took a sudden turn and things began to happen quickly. Without understanding these things, I might very likely have turned back, and I would not be where I am today, a disciple of Jesus Christ. So here are the lessons I had learned and what I believed to be true at this midway point in my journey.

- The world is not a logical place that is fully understandable by the application of reason.
- Complexity is the rule in nature, everywhere and always. Why this is true remained a mystery to me.
- Every answer we find in science leads to more questions, and no topic is ever exhausted; why this is so is not answerable from the data available.
- There are limits to the scientific approach to understanding and knowledge, and I had no idea how to go beyond them.

- I had no idea about how life arose or where it came from, and I learned that nobody else really did either.
- Evolution by natural selection is the best theory to explain how life became so diverse and complex, but it applies only to living organisms.
- Human beings are unique and a lot more special than any other living creature we know of. How they got that way, and what consciousness is all about, was still a mystery to me.
- I had no idea about the purpose of life—in general or for me in particular.

In short, I had reached the point where my certainty that there was nothing in the universe that could not be scientifically described was gone. Many of the arguments against theism seemed no longer valid. I now find it interesting that even though this became clear to me while I was still an atheist (I didn't believe in God), many anti-theists (those who believe theism is irrational or evil) continue to use those same tired arguments—the claim that belief in a deity is irrational, for example, or that miracles defy science. These claims cannot possibly hold water when science itself tells us that the universe is not rational and that much stranger things than miracles are everyday occurrences.

From Atheist to Agnostic

I was by no means a theist yet, but my atheism was badly shaken by these lessons from modern science. Perhaps the best word to describe my state of belief was *agnostic*. I simply didn't know, and I doubted I ever would. I was not at the point of believing in fairies, or magic, or God, or anything else of a spiritual nature, but I became more willing to at least think about what might be there beyond the stop signs of science. I still had a long way to go, and I was not done with learning more.

When I came to faith in God, it was not because I experienced a miraculous event. There was no unexplained recovery from a serious illness or accident; no prayer for the impossible come true. I did not witness anything out of the ordinary. But I did experience something. Something quite ordinary—no mystical flashes of light, no voice of God booming in my ears. Nothing like that. I simply had a dream.

Church

But I am getting ahead of myself. We aren't quite there yet. I was still a former atheist turned agnostic in my forties when, at the behest of a friend, I stepped into a church for the first time. I was full of dread as I crossed the threshold of an edifice that I had always thought represented not only ignorance and superstition but also much of the evil of human history: oppression, hypocrisy, reactionary anti-science, and endless corruption of power.

It was a Catholic church in a working-class section of Manhattan. In my nervousness, I expected people to point at me—surely they could tell I was there on false pretenses! I sat down, trying to be inconspicuous, and attempted to follow along. The church was large and full of people of all kinds. There were old and young, couples, families, a lot of folks by themselves. White, black, brown, and every possible color. Most were wearing ordinary street clothes. I could see that some looked to be in trouble. There were kids crying and some folks who didn't seem quite right—they were mumbling to themselves or even sleeping.

At a certain point, the priest leading the Mass said, "Give each other the sign of peace." The person next to me held out his hand and said, "Peace be with you." I shook his hand and saw that people were turning and shaking hands with others all around them. It was a pleasant surprise that no one grilled me as to why I was in the church or glared at me suspiciously. I felt like I could almost have belonged there. No one had any inkling that I was a renegade atheist, that I had no business sitting in the church, or that I was clueless about what was going on or why.

I listened to the priest when he gave the sermon. To my surprise, it was all about love. Nothing about damnation or hellfire. Nothing about what awaited sinners like me, nothing condemning or judgmental. It was about love for the righteous, love for sinners (like me), love for the lost, love for the searchers, love for the fallen, love for the lonely, love for the hopeless, love for all.

Years earlier I had read the Gospels as an academic exercise in the history of the times, so I was somewhat familiar with them. But the priest interpreted these stories in ways that related to everyday human life with an emphasis on human love and transcendence. I kept listening for some hidden subtext or subtle message, something about how scientists are destroying humanity, or how nonbelievers are doomed . . .

I never heard anything like that. I never heard a word spoken from hostility or righteous judgment. Instead, I heard about welcoming all people into the love of Christ, about how God the Father loves all His children. I heard about the power of faith, about forgiveness and redemption. I heard that all human beings are valuable in God's eyes and that Jesus treated sinners as people worthy of His love and attention.

Wait a minute, I thought, *this is not what I had learned about Christianity.* And I don't just mean from my parents—I had seen TV programs, read articles, absorbed books where the evils of Christianity were well featured. Hypocrisy, collaboration with Nazis, persecution of nonbelievers, and internecine warfare. I had been taught that this religion was all about intolerance and power, not about love. Could it be possible that the church, and perhaps the entire spectrum of Christian belief, had been given a bad rap? I knew such distortions of truth were possible and happened all the time. Perhaps my previously held view of Christianity as a corrupt system used for the manipulation and dominance of ignorant folk was at best only part of the truth . . .

All of this was interesting in an intellectual way, but it had nothing to do with faith. I felt distinctly uncomfortable during the Mass. I didn't actually say any prayers—I just listened. I was an observer. I had changed from a suspicious, hostile observer to a more sympathetic one, but I was still outside of the proceedings.

The Gospel of Matthew

Much later, I realized that Jesus had been calling me for a very long time, but I was deaf to the call. I remember the first time I heard (and rejected) the call of Jesus when I was about eighteen years old. My girlfriend at the time (who was secretly a Christian) brought me to see a classic film by Pier Paolo Pasolini called *The Gospel According to Saint Matthew*, which uses the words of the Gospel as its text. The soundtrack for the scene of the crucifixion and burial of Jesus is a solemn, heavy Russian chorus, which continues as Mary and John are arriving at the tomb three days after the death of Jesus.

The stone is suddenly rolled back, we see that the tomb is empty, and the music just as suddenly switches to a wonderful, joyous African Mass called the *Missa Luba*. The effect was overwhelming. I was overcome with a joyous emotion I could not identify . . . I shivered, and part of my mind (soul?) was secretly shouting "alleluia" while the rest of it was thrown into turmoil. This was a feeling I had been educated to fight against, and I did. I denied what I felt. I assumed it was just a trick of my emotional brain—my response to the music was fooling me into thinking there was something meaningful about the scene I had witnessed on the screen. After all, these were actors, this was a director's clever manipulation: in real life there is no soundtrack!

Although I never forgot that moment, I refused to acknowledge it as anything other than an episode of neurochemistry until much later. This flash of strange and forbidden beauty did not lead to my conversion, because at that age that would have been impossible for me. But now I know that what I had responded to was the beautiful truth that is behind the Gospel: the truth that God so loves us that He sent His only Son to us, to suffer and die, but then to rise from death and ascend to heaven. He was despised. He was rejected. And how many of us poor mortals have not been despised, have not been rejected? And yet we, too, are loved by the living God. This understanding of the wonder of the resurrection is beautifully conveyed in the film, and although I rationally rejected the idea, the joy of it permeated my being.

The Cliff and the Garden

I had another unforgettable call about a decade later, as a young man lost in many struggles of life. I was trying to succeed in my postgraduate education and having a hard time. My marriage at an early age was proving difficult, and I had lost all confidence in myself and my future. And then one night I had a dream (this is not the dream I mentioned earlier) that is very hard to describe, but I will try. I entered a building that was familiar to me, and I was walking between rows of people I knew who were greeting me, saying my name, and smiling. I felt loved, and I heard beautiful music. What I remember most about the dream was an intense and absolutely new feeling of complete and untarnished joy. It was the kind of joy you can see on the faces of people who have survived a tragedy, or who have won the trophy they have always longed for, or who have at long last found love.

When I woke up, that feeling of joy was still there, and it came with an understanding that whatever was happening to me now, somehow I would be victorious, I would succeed, I would be happy and experience that feeling of intense joy again and again. This was a revelation, perhaps even a vision of sorts. I never had a dream like that again, but I have always been able to summon that amazing feeling of utter happiness at will. I didn't know what was behind this dream when I had it (of course I do now), but I did not pursue that question. I had read about visions and ecstatic trances, and I just felt lucky that whatever rare neurological condition produces these events in people's brains had happened to me.

There may have been other calls to me, but if there were, I don't remember them, and I paid no heed to them. But then, in my early forties, when I was almost ready to receive the truth of God and His existence, I had two more dreams, separated by a couple of years.

In the first, I was trying to climb a sheer cliff (I am afraid of heights, so this was a terrifying dream), and I was holding on for dear life to a large rock that was jutting out from the cliff face. I couldn't move, and I thought I would fall at any minute. In panic, I called out for help, and a voice answered me: "Just let go." It seemed crazy, but the voice was insistent, so I did. And as I let go, the world turned ninety degrees, and instead of being vertical on a cliff face, I was lying on the ground and hugging a boulder. I let go of it and stood up, thinking, *That was easy!* I felt so relieved, so free and happy, that I started laughing. The man standing next to me, the man whose voice I had heard, said, "Yes, it is easy. All you have to do is let go."

In the second dream, I was outside a walled garden. I knew that in this garden there was to be found everything I had always been looking for, but there was no way I could climb over the wall to get in. I kept going around the walls, trying to climb up, falling down, and getting terribly frustrated. And then a man showed up and said to me, "What's wrong with you?" I explained I was trying to get into the garden but could not scale the wall. He smiled and said, "Then why not use the door?" He pointed to a door in the wall that I hadn't seen. I asked what I needed to do to gain entry. He answered, "Nothing—just open the door and go in." So I did.

What these dreams told me was that after having spent most of my life wishing I could be a believer, all I had to do was say, "OK, I'm a believer." And it worked. As soon as I let go of the rock (all the logical, intellectual, and cultural reasons to not believe) and entered the garden, I found myself tapping into a wellspring of Love that I had never thought I could be part of. And the miracle to me was that there was no test—there was no trial or rite of passage. It was right there, free for the taking. A gift. Not to be earned, just to be taken.

> He offers His love not as a reward
> but as a gift—a gift for anyone and
> everyone. To receive this gift, you
> need do only one thing: take it.

Shortly after the second dream, and after I had gone back to that first church a few times, I had an intuitive flash that what I had heard about God's love was true. He offers His love not as a reward but as a gift—a gift for anyone and everyone. To receive this gift, you need do only one thing: take it.

For years I had no idea that the gift was even there. And then I could see it: brightly lit, a package with a bow on top of bright wrapping paper. It looked really good, but I didn't trust it. I was sure it was a trap, something I wanted no part of. I thought, *Perhaps there is something good wrapped up in that package*, but I was afraid to take it and open it. Would I become beholden if I accepted this gift? Would I be disappointed? Maybe it was only another sweater or a tie. Would I feel let down?

I spent lots of time looking at the brightly wrapped package, sniffing around it like a cat sniffs a new toy. Sometimes I was tempted.

Sometimes I thought, *This can't be for me—I have done nothing to deserve any kind of gift.* Sometimes I thought, *Once I open this present, I can never unopen it,* and I was afraid.

And then, without me doing anything at all, it began to unwrap by itself. God thrust the gift of His love at me when I was ready, even though I didn't know I was ready. And there it was: beautiful, whole, perfect, eternal, wise, knowing, forgiving, loving. When I finally took it, I again felt the joy I had in the dream I experienced as a young man. That joy wells up in me frequently, and I know that I have reached the place I had hoped to reach when I first wondered what that vision might mean.

After the second dream, I began thinking that I was turning into a theist, but I still wasn't completely sure—I had many doubts. The whole idea of believing in God, let alone in Jesus Christ, was still embarrassing to me. After all, I was an active scientist, and I knew no Christians among my colleagues. (I later found out this wasn't true—I knew several, but they were keeping their Christianity quiet for fear of ridicule and worse.) I also had no intention of letting go of my scientific view of the world, and I thought that I would need to drop at least some of what I scientifically knew to be true if I really accepted Jesus. In other words, I was still on the threshold.

Crossing the Threshold

I crossed that threshold one day while driving along a highway in central Pennsylvania. I was searching for something to listen to on the radio, and I got hold of a Christian radio station. I listened to the preacher for a few minutes and realized the guy really had a great style of oratory. I also like to talk (would you believe it?), so I began imagining what I would say if I were preaching. I turned off the radio and without thinking at all about it, I began preaching a sermon to myself.

I pictured myself preaching somewhere in the South, standing on a stage, having been introduced as a brand-new minister of the faith. The words came smoothly and without hesitation. This is what I imagined myself saying as I drove along that highway:

Brothers and sisters, I would like to greet you and thank you for coming to hear me speak. I want to tell you who I am. I was not born around here. My family were not Christians. I was born in New York City, and my family were atheists from an ethnic Jewish background. My parents were not only atheists—they were communists. And when I say that, I don't mean that they voted Democrat or were ultraliberal. I mean they were actually members of the American Communist Party. They not only rejected God, they hated the idea of God. I never went to any religious service in my youth. In my early years, I was a left-wing radical. After going to college, I became a scientist like my father.

And so here I stand before you. A real-life communist scientist intellectual from New York City. And so you are probably thinking, What in God's name is that guy doing here, talking to a group of real Christians? *I will give two answers to that question. The first answer has three words. And the second answer has four words.*

The first answer, which you have heard many times, is this: "Jesus loves me." *The second answer is more powerful:* "Jesus loves even me." *Yes, I am standing here to tell you, brothers and sisters, that Jesus Christ, the Lord God made flesh, loves me, a commie atheist scientist sinner from godless New York City. I know this for a fact. And if that is true, which it is, who among you could He not love? Are you unworthy of His love? Have you sinned? You cannot be more unworthy than me, and I would bet that your sins are no worse than mine.*

Does it make sense that God would love me after decades

of my denial of His existence? No, it does not. I rejected Him, not once but over and over. And still His love is there. I worshipped idols; I denied my own soul. Doesn't matter. On a few occasions I even heard His call to me, and I ignored it and kept following my own path.

And yet, I can feel His love. How can I explain this? I can't. I never went to Sunday school; I never went to Hebrew school. I never prayed or read the Bible. I laughed at believers and cursed His churches. I don't deserve His forgiveness, or His love. I have not earned them. If God were just, I would be punished, not rewarded.

So what does this all mean? How can we make sense of this strange thing—that I, even I, am loved by the Lord? It must mean something. And yes, brothers and sisters, it does. It means that God is not only just but merciful, and His mercy is beyond our understanding. It means that He offers His love not as a reward but as a gift.

Whenever I go to church to pray, my prayer is always the same. It is a prayer of thanks. I thank God for His gift of love, and for His gift of my life. I see now that it is a wonderful life, full of turmoil, stress, people, adventure, peace, and joy. A human life. Another gift from God. So I stand here before you and say, "Thank You, Lord, thank You, Jesus Christ, who, as God made flesh, made it clear that You came not for the holy and the righteous only but for the lost, the sinners, the sick, and the wounded. And that You love all of us. Even me. Amen."

Those words came to my mind and were spoken in my mind out of thin air while driving on the Pennsylvania Turnpike. At one point I had to pull over because of the intense emotions I was feeling, and when I finished this mental sermon, I was crying. I was totally surprised by these words, since at that point I thought that if I were to say anything about God, it would have been about the chemical impossibility of nucleic acids interacting directly with amino acids or the statistical and philosophical hurdle of explaining the emergence of a genetic code from an informationally devoid universe.

The last thing I would have imagined talking about was God's love. In fact, that whole idea was not even in my conscious mind until I began "speaking" it. And that was in fact the moment when the gift wrapping came off, and I said, "Oh, what a lovely gift. Thank You, I will gladly accept it." I was a Christian, thanks to the grace of the Holy Spirit.

> I simply opened my heart, let go of whatever was in the way, and there it was. Grace.

And so, in my middle age, I had become one of those people I used to both envy and hold in contempt. Someone who was one with God and who had accepted Jesus as the redeemer of his life. I simply opened my heart, let go of whatever was in the way, and there it was. Grace. Free, and without strings. It wasn't even much of a burden to live a Christian life because I had been a fairly decent person beforehand, and I found that once you decide to follow Jesus, acts of charity and kindness just naturally happen. From you and to you.

A few years later, I was baptized and joined a congregation of the United Methodist Church. Not long after, the pastor asked me to deliver the message one Sunday: I was to talk about my journey to faith. I had to stand up at the lectern to give a real sermon! It was all I could do to remain standing as I (a veteran speaker from my years as a scientist) was trembling all over. I didn't make the same speech

I had preached to myself on the Pennsylvania Turnpike, not exactly, but I did talk about the miracle of God's love for sinners and those who had rejected Him. At that moment, I knew that the dream I had had as a young man, the vision of pure joy overtaking every fiber of my being, had come true.

PART 2

Issues and Questions

CHAPTER 10

But What About . . . ?

My journey from atheism to deep Christian faith was long and winding. Many of my friends, colleagues, and family knew nothing of my journey as it was happening, and when I finally came out as a Christian, I had a variety of reactions. Most people were pleasant, but some were astonished or concerned. But—they must have thought—I didn't seem to have become insane or delusional in other ways, so many who were at first worried eventually came to accept that this was a simple aberration and not a sign of mental degradation.

There was also, of course, an entire community of Christians who welcomed me. Many (like my wife) had followed parallel paths from atheism to faith. Some had gone the other way, from strict young-earth creationism and biblical literalism to evolutionary creationism (see chapter 12).

Among the group of folks who were less than impressed, several asked me questions that started something like this: "Wow, you really believe in all the God and Christ stuff! But what about . . . ?" followed by the standard litany of atheistic objections to faith, religion, Christianity, and God. I would answer these questions to the best of my ability. Since these answers are important to me, I will record them here, not only to justify to others my newfound joy in faith but also to reassure that part of my own soul that still needs to assuage long-held doubts and concerns.

> Faith is not the enemy of reason: it is the enemy of certainty. Doubts are a part of faith, and just like in science, lack of certainty is a strong stimulant for seeking truth.

I found that as I developed the answers, sometimes by doing the research necessary and sometimes by simply using logic and reason, my faith was strengthened. After all, reason and knowledge are allies of true faith. The popular myth that faith is what you have when you reject facts has it all wrong. Faith is not the enemy of reason: it is the enemy of certainty. Doubts are a part of faith, and just like in science, lack of certainty is a strong stimulant for seeking truth.

Here are some of the "But what about . . . ?" questions I have been asked, or I have asked myself, followed by the answers I came up with.

1. Haven't Christianity and other religions been responsible for most wars, cruelty, and oppression throughout history?

The common claim that Christianity (or religion in general) has caused the majority of human deaths perpetrated by other humans has no support in historical fact, as simple research can show. The believers of this myth usually cite the Crusades, the Inquisition, and sometimes wars waged in the name of Islam and acts of terrorism.

The Inquisition, while an awful chapter in church history, actually led to a relatively small number of deaths. Worse than both the

Inquisition and the Crusades were the Thirty Years' War and the French religious wars. But all of these pale in comparison to a series of Chinese civil wars and deliberately caused famines, the Mongol conquests, the two World Wars, the policies of Stalin and Mao, and colonialism, including the slave trade.

The following list is roughly in order, starting from the highest number of people killed. It includes the victims of famines that were a direct result of intentional policies.

World War II
Mao Zedong's policies
Mongol conquests
Three Kingdoms War (China)
Native American genocide
Stalin's policies
Mideast slave trade
Atlantic slave trade
Timur Lenk's wars
British Indian policies (mostly through famine)
World War I
Russian Civil War
Fall of Rome
Leopold II's Congo "Free State"
Thirty Years' War
Russian Czarist policies
Napoleonic Wars
Chinese Civil War
Crusades
French Wars of Religion

The majority of the events on this list—and the worst killers—had nothing to do with religion. Only the Thirty Years' War, the

Crusades, and the French Wars of Religion can be considered religious wars, and the label is somewhat controversial even for those (Catholic France joined the Protestant side in the Thirty Years' War, for example). If we add in all the other conflicts with a strong religious component, which include the Spanish Inquisition, the killing of "witches" in Europe, various Islamic wars and revolts, the Troubles of Northern Ireland, the Iranian Revolution, the Arab-Israeli conflict, and the Iran-Iraq War, a rough estimate of the total number of people killed is about ten million. (About 75 percent of these are from the Thirty Years' War, whose legitimacy as a purely religious conflict is questionable.)

Any number of people killed in religious warfare is a terrible thing. However, the claim that this toll represents most of the deaths, or even a major fraction of human-caused deaths, is absurd. The total number of people killed in the wars mentioned in the previous list is about 475,000,000. Even the most liberal estimate puts the percentage of people killed in religious conflicts compared to all human deaths from war and conflict at about 2 percent.

The fact that without any religious motivation close to five hundred million people have been murdered by their fellow human beings in the past two thousand years shows that people can be brutal and murderous toward their own species. Religion may not inoculate us against such tendencies, and religion has been a cause of or served as a rationale for conquest and genocide. However, there is absolutely no indication from the data that religion is the main cause of human-initiated suffering.

This does not excuse the religious violence we are so familiar with. But it isn't religion that is the culprit when it comes to human suffering—it is human greed, human lust for power, and human sin that we should blame. When such things take on a religious mantle, they are even more heinous and should be condemned by all.

2. Science is naturally atheistic—do any productive scientists believe in God?

This argument will come as a surprise to the many scientists who are professing Christians, as well as to the believing Muslims, Jews, and Hindus in the sciences. There have been many Nobel Prizes awarded to professing Christians and other believers in the hard sciences (physics, chemistry, physiology, and medicine). It is hard to come up with exact numbers since religious commitment is difficult to measure, and not everyone who considers their faith important in their lives speaks of it publicly. However, the various lists of Nobel Laureates suggest that at least twenty-five, and possibly up to a hundred, are professing Christians.

Besides the Nobel winners, famous scientists who considered themselves to be committed Christians throughout history include Francis Bacon, Blaise Pascal, Robert Boyle, Maria Cunitz, Gottfried Leibniz, Joseph Priestley, Alessandro Volta, André-Marie Ampère, Michael Faraday, James Clerk Maxwell, Gregor Mendel, Asa Gray, Lord Kelvin, George Washington Carver, Arthur Eddington, Lise Meitner, Kathleen Lonsdale, Francis Collins, John Polkinghorne, Jennifer Wiseman, and many more. One must indeed wonder how, if this particular argument were correct, there could possibly be so many outstanding, excellent, or even just moderately good scientists (a class I'm aiming for) who believe in God.

3. There are so many different religions and so many gods. They can't all be right, so why do you think yours is the only one that is true?

To answer this question, we must first understand the difference between gods and God. Yes, there are thousands of gods like Thor, Poseidon, and Krishna, but they are qualitatively different from the concept of one transcendent, immaterial God, omnipotent and omniscient, who alone is the Creator and Ruler of the universe. My God is not a superhuman, magical being with special powers who otherwise acts and thinks much like we do. My God is not a god of magic who routinely changes the workings of reality to suit His whims. The one true God is outside of space and time.

There are three religions that claim to worship one God: Judaism, Christianity, and Islam. Of these, Christianity is unique in its triune approach to the Godhead, with Jesus Christ as the incarnation of God who came to earth and sacrificed Himself for our redemption.

Of these three monotheistic religions, I believe in Christianity. This is true not because I was brought up in the faith, but because I was free to choose which religion made the most sense to me intellectually and which one I had a direct spiritual experience with. Christianity fit both of those bills. Like Jews and Muslims, I worship God as the Creator of the universe and as the Lawgiver. I also believe (based on both objective and subjective evidence) that God chose to walk among us in the form of a man and spread His message of love, meaning, and salvation to all humans.

4. But science is free and open, while religion is dogmatic and rigid. How can you stand to obey religious commandments and rules with no chance of challenging them?

The claim that religion is dogmatic and doctrinal by nature has long been a favorite objection against religion. It's odd that some atheists don't seem to see the contradiction between this argument and the preceding one: each cancels the other. The reason there are so many varieties of Christian faith, for example, is exactly because of the diversity of religious ideas and practices, and the rebellion of so many great minds against stifling and rigid purity of thought. Such rebellions and diversity would not be possible if Christianity or any other faith really were a rigid and unbending dogma. But it isn't only the splitting of denominations to form new ones that argues against this line. I have not been a Christian for many decades, but

I have already seen changes in the United Methodist Church, and before that in the Roman Catholic Church (which was supposed to be the most doctrinaire of all). I would even say that as regards willingness to consider new ideas and make changes in established doctrine, many religions are not much behind science.

5. How can you reconcile science based on clear facts with faith based on nothing?

The scientific method is also based on articles of faith that all scientists must agree on, although many have forgotten that this is so. One such article of faith is that a fact proven to be true will always be true, in all time and all places. This statement might appear to be self-evident to some people, but it really isn't—it is a statement of faith that in fact has sometimes turned out to be false. There are some facts that are *not* equally true in all times and places, and some facts that *seemed* to be proven true were not really proven. But for the most part, this unspoken article of faith in the nature of reality works, and we use it all the time.

I did not need to invent a microprocessor, since I have faith that my computer will work. (Speaking of misplaced faith!) If I read a paper that presents experimental results that surprise me, I might doubt them until I see that several other laboratories get the same results. At that point, I will have faith that the answer is true without having to "see for myself." Faith in the results of experimental (or theoretical) science stems from the willingness to *believe*, as first articulated by Francis Bacon, that what we observe (empirical evidence) is more real than what we merely think or imagine or even what we have heard from authorities. This understanding was the beginning of the Enlightenment and the birth of science as we know it.

There are miraculous interventions in my life that cannot be explained in any other way than the act of a loving God. That is the data. And I have faith in that data, just as I have faith in the data I see published when it is replicated over and over. Being open to such data, to signals, to wisdom, to facts, to the world as it comes to us, is the best way to blend faith with intellect in order to come to a true understanding of reality.

Later, I found another source of data, which, like scientific data, is open to interpretation. That source is the text of Scripture. I had already been strongly moved by the little I'd read (such as the Gospel of Matthew), but now I began to look into the rest of the Bible, which brings us to the next question.

6. But what about the Bible? You can't believe in both the Bible and in the scientific version of reality. They contradict each other continuously!

The Bible is not an automotive repair instruction manual or a book of recipes. It is a work of literature that contains knowledge, wisdom, stories, rules, poetry, and beauty. Our Lord Jesus told stories and parables. Why would He do that if He didn't want us to think and interpret?

I think that many conservative evangelicals who reject evolution feel that they are defending the very substance of Christian faith. I have read theologian Albert Mohler and others who claim that if we accept evolution, we are on the slope toward rejecting everything in the Bible and in danger of losing the moral compass given to us by God.[1]

I don't at all agree, but I can understand this concern. If the Bible is our lifeboat in a stormy sea of moral and mortal danger, then poking even the smallest hole in it can seem terrifying. For this reason, it is vital to demonstrate that acceptance of evolution is not a disputation of the authority of the Bible. Instead, it relies on alternative interpretations of God's inspired Word.

In *The Language of Science and Faith*, Karl Giberson and Francis Collins stress this point. They quote Augustine (as quoted by

Galileo), arguing that humans cannot be certain that their understanding of what they read in the Bible is correct. Biblical interpretation has always been a mainstay of Christian theology. There is a
long history of alternative interpretations of Scripture.

The slippery slope argument is potent because there have been
examples of liberal theologians who have argued away some of the
basic tenets of Christian faith. But embracing evolution and the rest
of science does not in any way diminish our faith in Jesus Christ as
the Messiah, or in the resurrection, original sin, free will, and our
redemption by Christ. On the contrary, science enhances faith, and
the moral basis of the Bible's teachings and its historical witness are
in no danger from scientific revelations.

We are all in the same boat, and the sea is indeed stormy. But by
accepting evolution and the rest of science, we are not poking holes
in the boat's structure—we are instead strengthening it. Fear is and
always was the enemy, and faith in God is our protector and guide
against fear.

But are we as Christians allowed to interpret the Bible any way
we please? Here is a quote from someone far more qualified than I
am to answer that question.

> The Bible is not a natural science textbook, nor does it
> intend to be such. It is a religious book, and consequently
> one cannot obtain information about the natural sciences
> from it. One cannot get from it a scientific explanation of
> how the world arose; one can only glean religious expe-
> rience from it. Anything else is an image and a way of
> describing things whose aim is to make profound realities
> graspable to human beings. One must distinguish between
> the form of portrayal and the content that is portrayed. The
> form would have been chosen from what was understand-
> able at the time—from the images which surrounded the

people who lived then, which they used in speaking and in thinking, and thanks to which they were able to understand the greater realities. And only the reality that shines through these images would be what was intended and what was truly enduring. Thus Scripture would not wish to inform us about how the different species of plant life gradually appeared or how the sun and the moon and the stars were established. Its purpose ultimately would be to say one thing: *God* created the world. . . .

The story of the dust of the earth and the breath of God, which we just heard, does not in fact explain how human persons come to be but rather what they are. It explains their inmost origin and casts light on the project that they are. And, vice versa, the theory of evolution seeks to understand and describe biological developments. But in so doing it cannot explain where the "project" of human persons comes from, nor their inner origin, nor their particular nature. To that extent we are faced here with two complementary—rather than mutually exclusive—realities.

—Pope Benedict XVI[2]

It isn't only my opinion that the Bible is not to be taken as a science manual. It is also the opinion of the former leader of the Roman Catholic Church, as well as of Christians in the majority of Protestant denominations and the Eastern Orthodox Church.

So how do we decide what is to be taken literally and what is to be assumed as an allegory, metaphor, parable, or illustration? This is not an easy question, and I believe that we each must work to find the answer, perhaps with guidance from others—pastors, priests, theologians, or other Christians, who themselves will differ. But this is not doing science—it is the practice of faith, which is decidedly *not* a blind obedience to some list of behaviors and beliefs. Faith is dynamic, both within churches and within each individual believer, always changing, evolving, and growing. It requires discernment, learning, prayer, understanding, listening, and even experimentation. Much like science (except for the prayer part—usually).

As theologians Alister McGrath, John Walton, N. T. Wright, Denis Lamoureux, and others tell us, the Bible needs to be understood in the context of what people knew at the time it was written. I have heard complaints that Genesis 1 isn't scientifically accurate. Of course it isn't—how could it be? If God inspired ancient humans to write the text, how could He have possibly communicated to them what we now know to be scientifically factual material?

Let's imagine that God had dictated to an inspired human scribe something like this:

> In the beginning, there was a state of nothingness: no space, no time, no matter, no energy, just Me. I created the universe through a singularity in which there was the creation and rapid expansion of space-time. I made it so there was a period of inflation during which the universe expanded faster than the speed of light. After a while, the universe got less dense, and I allowed photons to escape the dense cloud of matter, and so there was light. Four forces emerged from the first microseconds of the universe, including gravity. I set the physical constants for these forces just right so that the universe would come out perfectly to allow for the formation of galaxies, stars, carbon, planets, and, eventually, life.

The ancient listener, who had no idea what a singularity, space-time, photons, or galaxies were would very likely have written down God's words as best as he understood them. Perhaps the word *expansion* evoked the image of a river overflowing its banks. He probably heard the part about the initial absence of light, but then light was also created. So he was inspired to write:

> In the beginning, God created the heavens and the earth. The earth was without form and void, and darkness was over the face of the deep. And the Spirit of God was hovering over the face of the waters.
>
> And God said, "Let there be light," and there was light. (Gen. 1:1–3)

The following tale might serve to imagine how the original composition of the Bible happened, and why it's not an "easy" read.

A Fable About the Bible

"You guys are kidding, right?"

"What do you mean?"

"What do I mean? You are collaborating on a book. One of you writes the first chapter, the other writes the second. And so on."

"Right. That's what we did."

"Great. But tell me something. Did either of you read what the other one wrote?"

The two authors looked at each other, then back at the editor.

"Um, well, I mean not in, you know, detail," said the first author (we will call him P). "But I thought she did a fine job."

"Really? Interesting. You thought she did a fine job. You [pointing at P] talk about humans being 'male and female, He created them' on day six, and your friend here [pointing at Ms. J] talks about some guy made of dust and a woman made from his rib. Did you happen to notice that the two of you wrote two chapters for one book (and a very important book because the plan was to put it in the beginning of the whole anthology) that not only are inconsistent but contradict each other?" The editor was raising his voice.

After a brief silence, J spoke up. "I cannot change a word or a jot of what I wrote." (I don't know what a jot is, but that's what she said.) "Everything I wrote was inspired directly from God."

"Me too," said P.

The editor threw his pencil down on the desk in exasperation. "Look, we all work for the same team here. If you insist, I will send these two chapters upstairs, but I am sure you are both facing some major rewrites."

A short time later, God called the editor for an audience.

"Yes, Lord."

"Great job on the Genesis book. I love those first two chapters."

"Um, thank you, Lord, but . . . I mean, are You sure? Don't they strike You as . . . oh, I don't know, a bit discordant with each other?"

"Well, they were written by two people, each with different styles, so yeah, they are diverse all right. That's exactly what I was going for when I assigned those two to do this."

"But, Lord, I am sorry to say this, and I mean no offense, but . . . well, they contradict each other. I mean, there are two completely different versions of the creation of humankind."

The Lord smiled.

"I think you are a great editor. But there is something you need to learn about this whole project. I have chosen some wonderful writers with great faith and passion. I have chosen some other writers who are not that wonderful, but whose faith and passion are even deeper. Every word they write is inspired by Me but written by them. If I think they got it wrong, I have them change it. So you never have to worry that I don't approve of what they hand in to you. You can consider all of it to be preapproved.

"Now, I will also tell you that I don't care about having a book that is an easy read. It is not going to be something you can read in two weeks at the beach and then forget the plot and the names of the characters. It is not going to have a single cliché in it. At times it will not make sense at all. It will have violence and poetry, love and anger; it will be exciting and more boring than a cookbook. It will appear to contradict itself, like in those two chapters, but it won't really. It will contain enigmas, puzzles, challenges, clues, mysteries, allegories, history, and lots of characters. Sometime the heroes will seem to be villains, and even I will come off as unpleasant at times."

"But Lord, I thought You wanted this book, or this series of books, to stand the test of time, to inspire generations of people, to be spread throughout the world and translated into hundreds of languages, and to give comfort, advice, and inspiration to Your people. Why would You want this book to be so hard to figure out?"

"Because that is exactly how it will stand the test of time and be spread throughout the world. This book, My book, will be read and not understood until someone works hard enough to get it. It will be discussed and debated. And people will think and learn. Believe Me, I know what I'm doing. I am God, after all.

"Oh, and by the way. Those first two chapters of Genesis that you are worried about?"

"Yes, Lord?"

"Don't worry, they don't contradict each other at all. There is a hidden message in there that might be a bit obscure, but My people will find all kinds of new ways to understand the world, and when they do, they will figure everything out, including My book. They are good at figuring things out—it's what they like to do. That's one of the reasons I love them. They will think and argue and do experiments—"

"Do what, Lord?" the editor interrupted.

"Never mind, you will find out. Anyway, eventually they will

get it all, and then when they praise Me and the glory of My creation, they will really mean it, for its glorious splendor will amaze
and delight them."

The editor sighed. Sometimes he wished God was not so
wise, but then He wouldn't be God, would He?

"OK, Lord, I understand. I will let it all go as I get it."

"Good. I'm glad to hear it. Because if you think Genesis is
tough, wait until you see what D hands in."

What is intriguing about the Genesis account of creation is not
how much of it is "wrong" (at least according to our present understanding), but how much is right. Unlike other creation stories,
Genesis talks of creation taking place over a period of time, marked
in divisions of days. God did not poof everything into existence in
one shot. The order of creation also shows an uncanny similarity
to what we now know, with vegetation preceding sea creatures, followed by animals and lastly human beings. These were profound
insights that would not have been a natural way for ancient peoples
to think.

The other big problem with attacking Genesis for being scientifically inaccurate is that we don't really know what is truly accurate in scientific cosmology. It wasn't long ago that science held to
a steady-state universe (see chapter 7). We can only imagine what
scientific cosmology will tell us about the origin of the universe five
thousand years from now.

The main point is that Genesis has a different purpose than giving a scientifically accurate account of how creation happened. As
John Walton and others have said, the message of Genesis is that
God created everything that exists, including the moon and the
sun, which people at the time thought of as gods. And the godly acts
of creation have as much to do with making order (separating one
thing from another) as with de novo creation of matter and energy.

7. But don't most Christians believe that everything in the Bible is literally true, and therefore evolution and a lot of other science is wrong?

According to a recent Pew Study, roughly a two-thirds majority of Christians in the world accept evolution and science in general. Only a few American Protestant denominations take an official stand against evolution (along with other religious groups such as Jehovah's Witnesses, Mormons, and a few others[3]), and even those denominations have members who personally hold views compatible with evolution. Admittedly, there are members of other denominations who believe in a young earth and think that "creation science" is a real alternative to evidence-based science.

Even in the United States, where young-earth creationism is more widespread than in the rest of the world, a clear majority (about 55 percent) reject the interpretation of Genesis as a science textbook and the calculation that the universe was created six thousand years ago. This includes the great majority of Lutherans, Presbyterians, Methodists, Calvinists, Catholics, Episcopalians, Nazarenes, and Anglicans, as well as large numbers of Baptists and nondenominational Christians.[4]

It should also be noted that nobody *really* takes the Bible strictly literally. Answers in Genesis (AiG), one of the most passionate defenders of young-earth creationism, has interpreted Genesis 2:7–25 as a detailed retelling of Genesis 1:26–27, but that is not stated in the text. They claim the world is six thousand years old, but that is an interpretation of genealogies, not literally stated. The idea that Adam was the first man is also an interpretation, not something the text declares. And the question of who Cain's wife was, and who the people were he feared would kill him, gets an answer from AiG that involves a great deal of incest among Adam's children, an interpretation I find morally and spiritually problematic. The point is that everyone interprets Scripture, even if they don't admit it.

8. Christianity is based on miracles, while science is based on reason and evidence. How can a scientist believe in miracles?

The brilliant writer C. S. Lewis argued in his book *Miracles* that miracles represent divine interventions beyond natural laws. In other words, a miracle is God driving beyond the stop sign (chapter 8). In order to consider this idea, we must accept the principle that there *is* something more than nature, that purely natural, material causes do not explain *everything*, and that a benevolent Creator exists outside of our natural world who intervenes (albeit rarely) in our reality through miracles.

This would mean that philosophical naturalism—the idea that only the natural world exists and that natural causes explain everything—is false. But how can that be when science relies on a naturalist assumption? Science can investigate only natural causes and therefore assumes natural causes in its methodology (*methodological* naturalism), but it requires no *philosophical* commitment to the idea that nothing beyond those natural causes could possibly exist.

Lewis and other philosophers have made a very good case that philosophical naturalism is wrong, using what is called "the argument from reason." It goes more or less like this: Naturalism requires that human thought, like everything else, is derived from a natural cause, namely neurochemical processes in the brain. Reason is based on inference from observed facts, but at the same time it derives from the natural causation of neuronal firing, which is not traceable to any purely rational cause. Therefore, reason is based partly on a nonrational process (human neurophysiology). In fact (as many atheists are fond of saying), human beliefs can be explained by such nonrational causes. But if that is true (and if naturalism is true), we have a problem. A rational conclusion cannot be based on a nonrational premise, so if the human mind itself is not rational, it is impossible for us to infer beliefs rationally. If we believe—like almost everyone does—that we humans are capable of reason, then it logically follows that naturalism cannot be universally true. As Lewis explained, "Reason is simply the unforeseen and unintended by-product of mindless matter at one stage of its endless and aimless becoming. Here is flat contradiction. They ask me at the same moment to accept a conclusion and to discredit the only testimony on which that conclusion can be based."[5]

Another way to look at this issue relates to the problem of consciousness, as discussed in chapter 6. If consciousness is an illusion, "nothing but" the meaningless firing of certain neural circuits—as would be the case if pure naturalism were true—then human reason, a product of that illusory consciousness, would itself be illusory, and it would be impossible for humans to actually *know* anything to be true based on reason, which, of course, would be a product of that illusory consciousness.

This would mean that only computers could possess any real knowledge about the universe. At some time in the future, we might reach a point where computers are able to arrive at a complete, perfect understanding of everything. And that would actually prove my point: computers rely on an agency outside their natural world—human minds—to be programmed and to receive input data. Their capacity for reason originates with that outside agency. Analogously, we humans derive our capacity for reason from a rational source outside of our universe—God.

This argument against pure naturalism is quite persuasive to me, but of course it isn't to philosophical naturalists and atheists. The point is that there is a consistency in believing in reason and believing in the existence of an omniscient and omnipotent God outside of our universe, who created our world and continues to sustain it using the laws of nature, and who at times goes beyond those laws to use what we call miracles.

There is another approach to miracles that I began thinking about before I accepted the existence of God. This approach is neither naturalist nor supernaturalist—it is based on the observation that sometimes extraordinary things happen. These events do not violate the laws of nature, but their probabilities are so low that one is struck by a sense of wonder when witnessing them. Everyone has heard of such occurrences, and many have experienced them. Sometimes these events happen in a way to produce a great benefit to people, and often they lead to an epiphany of faith.

A large proportion of such "miracles" are done by people. Acts of immense courage, self-sacrifice, and charity are common in all cultures and all societies. Can they be reduced to behavior stemming from evolutionary imperatives and neural reflexes? Of course they can, if one wants to do that. I prefer to think of them as something much more than that, as signs of the divinity reflected in our image. As I said in chapter 6, we are used to miracles, and we call them human nature.

9. The Gospel accounts are not consistent and can even contradict each other, so how can we know that the story of Jesus Christ is real?

Some people have argued that it is hard to believe in the life and work of Jesus Christ because there are many inconsistencies in the written witness accounts between the four Gospels. I have never understood this objection. It goes against everything we know about historical methodology and the analysis of texts, and it never seems to be applied to any other ancient documents, only to the Bible. Of course there are contradictions—we would expect there to be contradictions. Four witnesses to any event will recall and interpret things differently, and they will give conflicting and contradictory assessments of what happened. If they all said the same thing, it would be highly likely that they were either coached or they conspired to make the whole thing up. Imagine if the four Gospels were perfectly in line with each other. It would then be assumed that all were copied from one source—and with only one source, the story would be less, not more, believable.

In other words, perfect agreement between different accounts of an event suggest collusion and possibly deliberate falsehood. Wildly differing accounts could mean that one or more of the witnesses are lying. Small differences in accounts suggest no collusion, and such accounts are likely to contain the most truth.

For example, Mark provides much more detail than Matthew about the recruitment of Simon, John, and James as the first disciples. Does this mean that it never happened or that the two accounts are contradictory? Of course not. When I read the Gospels for the first time, while still an atheist, I was struck by how truthful they appeared, even to the point of admitting embarrassing details, and it never occurred to me that the Jesus story was a legend, even though I didn't believe He was God.

The Gospels portray events that happened two thousand years ago. I was a direct witness to some historical events that transpired only forty years ago (about the same amount of time that passed from Christ's resurrection until the stories were being written down). Some of those events were witnessed by dozens of reporters and even captured on film. Yet I have seen that my own memory of those events doesn't always match all that well with the versions I have seen in the media and heard from other people. This is a well-known phenomenon in historical scholarship.

I don't think we need worry whether the story of Jesus as given in the four Gospels is true. The evidence is pretty strong that it is.

10. And what about evil? How could such a good, loving God allow so much evil in the world?

That is the hardest question of all, and I have devoted part of the next chapter to trying to answer it.

CHAPTER 11

Love and Freedom, Chance and Will

WHEN MY DAUGHTER was about four, she had two dolls. She loved to play with them, one in each of her hands, by having them talk to each other. She provided all the dialogue, but you could tell which doll was supposed to be talking because she would move it by shaking the appropriate hand. Once, in the middle of such a conversation, she looked up at me and said, "Daddy, I wish these dolls would come alive and do their own talking. That would be much more fun." I nodded and suggested that when she grew up, she might have her own children, who would, in fact, say and do whatever they wanted to. She seemed to like this idea at first, but then she frowned. "But what if I don't like what they say and do?"

The dilemma of total control versus the allowance of freedom is one we have all faced. Parents, bosses, governments, and, if I dare say it, God Himself wrestle with it. It's an important issue, one of the most important, since it is fundamental to discussions of why the universe is the way it is, why there is evil, and how God interacts with His creatures.

One of the biggest issues that people have with Christianity, and with belief in a benevolent and loving God in general, is the source of evil. In addition to human moral evil, there are natural disasters and all the things that happen to us every day that make it appear that God doesn't exist or doesn't care about us or is perhaps not as good as we are supposed to think. "If God is good and omnipotent, why would He allow evil to exist?" atheists (and even believers) frequently ask. That is a very fair question—one that buttressed my own atheism for decades.

Theodicy, the attempt to account for evil while retaining a Christian understanding of God, is probably the thorniest part of theology. Many authors have tackled the question of evil. Thomas Jay Oord in *The Uncontrolling Love of God* emphasizes God's inherently noncoercive love in relation to creation. The physicist-theologian George Murphy, in his book *The Cosmos in the Light of the Cross*, discusses how a theology of the cross means coming to terms with the death and suffering of Christ as a redemptive act on the part of the Deity. And, of course, the Gospel of John shows that death is not the absolute evil that many feel it is: "Truly, truly, I say to you, unless a grain of wheat falls into the earth and dies, it remains alone; but if it dies, it bears much fruit" (12:24).

The Good Creation

The first question to consider is whether evil exists in prehuman nature. Imagine you are watching a nature show on TV, and you see a fox hunting. The fox kills a baby rabbit and carries it off in its teeth. You squirm at the horror of this killing of the innocent, adorable bunny, and you think of the fox as the manifestation of evil. But the next scene shows the fox bringing the kill to a litter of baby foxes, who are starving. The mother, half starving herself, eats none of it but makes sure each of her offspring gets fed. The contrast between the two scenes is hard to resolve without some further thought about the biological world.

Could God have created a world without predation? Although I believe that God is omnipotent, I would answer no to this question. There are many things that God does not do in this universe. God does not allow for the existence of a perpetual-motion machine, or for light to go faster than a fixed speed, or for gravity to be reversed, or for people to travel back in time. While all these things are *possible for God*, they would violate His laws of nature, destroying the very concept of an orderly, lawful universe that is the hallmark of His creation. It is in this sense that Christianity is diametrically opposed to magic: in a magical universe, there are no laws, and anything, including the absence of any suffering, is possible.

What about predation? The existence of death is a critical part of life on earth. This did not have to be true. There could be planets or universes where life is immortal, non-evolving, and non-reproducing (these must go together). But on this planet, a key aspect of life is evolution, and evolution requires the death of all individual living creatures. It might seem a high price to pay, but evolution is the best (perhaps only) way to allow for the development of large animals with complex nervous systems. So, in order to have thinking creatures like us, who are free to worship God, there must be evolution, and there must be death.

Why couldn't all animals be vegetarians? After all, when a rabbit eats some clover, nothing is hurt, nothing dies. Why didn't God step in and create a world where no animal ever killed any other animal for food? This is the version of the Eden myth proposed by most young-earth creationists. According to this view, before the fall of Adam by sin, there was no death or suffering. Unfortunately, this cannot work in the real-world ecology we know. A stable and balanced ecological system requires predation of plant eaters. If there were no predation, overpopulation would ensue, followed by mass starvation and possibly the extinction of all animals. Scenarios like this, when predatory species were removed from an ecology, have been seen in nature, and the outcome is never good. When wolves were returned to Yellowstone National Park, the entire ecosystem, even the geology of rivers, quickly regained health and balance.

But what about the other evil of natural history—tsunamis, earthquakes, diseases, and so on? I think the explanation for the fact that our world is not perfect is that it has to actually work. The existence of tectonic plates helped the early earth trap carbon, stabilized the climate, and allowed complex life to exist, but once you have tectonic plates, you get earthquakes, volcanoes, and tsunamis. Christian writer Jon Garvey has found that the concept of a fallen earth is not a very old Christian doctrine. He discusses the history and theology of this teaching in his book *God's Good Earth.*

This is indeed a *good* creation, meaning that it works very well. It is we humans who need to strive for the moral goodness that does not exist in evolutionary-driven biological nature. Biological evolution stopped being the main driving force for human progress and development when we became fully modern (or in biblical terms, it stopped with Adam and Eve, the beginning of morality). At that point the dominant force for change became cultural evolution, in all its aspects (see chapter 7).

I have to admit that my own approach to theodicy is not theologically sophisticated. It relies on my observation that we tend to view reality in relative terms. I'm one of those who generally see the world as a very good place, despite the reality of horrors and suffering. To explain why I have become an optimist, I need to introduce the idea I call the *default position*—and show how it colors our perceptions of reality.

The Default Position

I once knew a woman who was not happy with the house she lived in. It was on a quiet street in a small town, with a backyard, a driveway and a garage, a front and back porch, a living room, dining room, eat-in kitchen, three bedrooms upstairs, full basement, fireplace, and studio. She felt it was too small, and she wanted to find a bigger house, similar to the one where she had grown up in a wealthy sub- urb. To her, the default position was to live in a house that was big enough to not be exactly sure how many rooms there were, to feel that space was almost unlimited. She felt she had descended from her default position.

It so happened that I was involved in an organization doing charity work in the resettling of refugees in the same town. I was a peripheral player, mostly doing grunt work like hauling furniture and helping fix up an apartment that the group had rented for a family about to arrive from Russia. I also did a lot of driving. I drove the family from the airport to their new apartment. They were a husband and wife, the man's mother, and a teenage daughter—the only one who spoke any English.

A couple of people from the organization met the family in the apartment, and I helped bring their suitcases inside. They were shown the master bedroom, the living room, the smaller bedroom, and the kitchen. The woman looked around carefully in the kitchen and the other rooms, speaking to the daughter in a low voice. She didn't seem terribly pleased, although she smiled politely. When she got to the bathroom, she said something that sounded like a ques- tion. The leader of our group asked the daughter what she had asked. The girl asked shyly, "Is one bathroom?" Our leader replied that yes, unfortunately we could only afford an apartment with one bath- room. He then asked her what her mother thought of the place. There ensued a brief family discussion, and then the girl said, "Is very nice apartment. My mother say kitchen small, but OK. But please, we like to ask, which room is ours? And how many families to share?"

When we were able to explain that no other families were shar- ing the place, that it was entirely for them, they were incredulous, and they all began to cry with wonder. The man sank to his knees to pray. We were all hugged by each of them, and of course we were all crying as well.

The Russian family's default position was to live in a single bedroom in a two-bedroom apartment shared with three other families.

The loftier one's default position, the more likely one is to be unhappy and upset with reality. Those with a humbler default position often find great joy in the relative happiness they find. We all have different default positions, for our own lives and also for the status of humanity. The default position for many Christians and others is that the world should be good and suffering limited or nonexistent. For some, the default position for humanity is one of universal peace, happiness, brotherhood—a good, clean, and happy world, where there is no illness, sorrow, or pain. Anything less than that is unacceptable and a source of anger, frustration, and despair. For me that world is a goal, but not the default position.

Partially because of my upbringing and partially because of my later reading about human prehistory as well as the dark chapters of recent history, my own default position of the status of humanity was much grimmer than either scenario described earlier. I used to think of the default position for the life of a human being as one of constant struggle to survive.

Growing up as an atheist, in a very materialistic and hyperrational household, I learned that it isn't the bad things that are rare but the good things. I was not surprised when I learned that a young friend of mine was dying; instead, I was amazed to hear that another friend had overcome a disability to achieve success. I was quite ill as a teenager, but I never questioned God since I "knew" there was no God. I accepted that such things were bound to happen, and I was simply unlucky. And then when I recovered, I felt that luck had swung in my favor. But I knew not to expect such lucky breaks. My default position was that I lived in a cold and dark place. Suffering? Of course there is suffering, how could there not be?

As a believer, I still see the pain and misery of so much of humanity, but now I also see the hope promised by Jesus Christ for a new life of joy and peace. As a youth, I heard this attitude in the music and words of African American Christians in the civil rights movement, but I could not understand what they were talking about. Now, praise God, I do. Like the Russian family, I now sink to my knees in joyful prayer at any hint of light or warmth in what I used to think was a harsh, uncaring universe. Starting from such a dark place, it is no wonder that when I discovered the beauty of nature and the reality of God's good gifts to humanity, I became a joyful optimist. While some argued whether the glass was half empty or half full, for me the default position was an empty glass, so now I am filled with wonder at the miracle that there is any water in the glass at all. This is why all my prayers are of thanksgiving.

God Loves the World

While life has always been hard, history tells us that humankind has made steady and amazing progress in the way we live. When human beings learned how to fish about twenty-five thousand years ago, it was a big step up from the original human default position. So were agriculture, houses, writing, music, and art—not to mention technology like air-conditioning, airplanes, computers, and cell phones. We have continued to raise our default position for thousands of years. And that is a remarkable thing—no other animal has ever done that. Look around you. Almost everything you see is a wondrous miracle of human undertaking to transcend our default position.

And yet in every age, people think they are living in the worst of times. I have lived long enough to know that we tend to forget how bad the "good old days" really were. One cure for malaise about the state of human life at the present is to study the history of Europe in the ninth or fourteenth centuries, or even as recently as 1940–41. For my grandfather, who crossed Europe on foot carrying nothing but the tools of his trade, my life—not to mention my son's life—would seem like heaven. For him, being able to buy food in a store and to eat something besides potatoes for every meal seemed like a dream when he arrived in the United States. And yet how often do I really mean it when I thank God for my dinner of steak, vegetables, and dessert that my ancestors (and yours) could only imagine in their dreams? We take the good in our lives for granted and complain about the bad unless we remind ourselves of the ever-present default position.

We do suffer, and misery is real. God has given us many gifts to overcome our suffering, and the most important is the example of His Son, our Savior Jesus Christ, who suffered more than most of us. Christ tells us that like Him, we are destined for a final victory over suffering in eternal life because God is good.

> I saw that the world, the world as it is, is
> not a terrible place but a place of beauty,
> of intricate design, a cleverly woven fabric
> of amazing order and perfect harmony.

When I understood that Christ is real and that God loves the world, I felt that a beautiful light had been turned on. Now I could see that all those good things I had thought were rare examples of extraordinary luck were really blessings from God. And the more I could see, the more blessed everything appeared. I saw that the world, the world as it is, is not a terrible place but a place of beauty, of intricate design, a cleverly woven fabric of amazing order and perfect harmony. As a biologist, I became and remain transfixed at the miraculous, unending complexity of life; as a person, I fell in love with the wonder of the human spirit. I have seen courage, humor, love, creativity, passion, and devotion in so many of my fellow creatures, far beyond what I would ever have expected from my original default position. The beauty of this world and the magnificence of the living creatures in it led me to thank the Creator every day for allowing me to experience such joy and behold such wonders. I don't deny suffering, of course. But I embrace joy. That suffering exists is no mystery for me. That joy exists is a surprising, divine gift to us all.

We have all heard of how people come together to help each other in times of disaster or great evil. I experienced this myself in New York City on September 11, 2001, and on the days that followed. While there was a strong sense of anger at those who had perpetrated the attack, the overwhelming mood in the city was one of mutual caring and love for all those affected. I saw this in the way people welcomed strangers stranded in town into their apartments, and in the volunteers who brought food and water to the firefighters working at the site. I saw it in the church I went to on the Friday after the attack, when a full house prayed, held candles, spoke the names of their lost loved ones, and comforted each other. I saw it in the street musicians who played and sang songs of peace and love in the parks to try to bring healing to the people. Love and kindness were everywhere; courtesy and respect replaced the usual New York curtness and suspicion.

Such blessings in the midst of despair are a common feature of human life, and while they do not in any way cancel the horror of the human act or natural disaster that caused the despair, they are worth acknowledging and celebrating, for this is also part of our human condition.

Deterministic Versus Stochastic Universe

In chapter 2, we saw that purely chance events based on probabilities are the hallmark of quantum physics. Outside the quantum world, truly random (stochastic) events are rare. As you might remember from my card-flipping story, some phenomena that appear to be random (controlled by nothing but chance) are not really stochastic. They seem that way because there does not seem to be any method we can use to exert control over them or guess their outcome. Events that are not stochastic, even if they appear to be random in nature, are called deterministic. *Determinism* simply means that there is some set of causes that determine the precise outcome of the event, and if we knew all those causes *and* had an infinite capacity to calculate, we would be able to accurately predict what is going to happen. This is true for chaotic phenomena like the weather and the stock market—they are deterministic, but our ability to predict their behavior, even in the short term, is very limited.

A complex and unpredictable universe is also an interesting universe. Think of the enormous complexity of space with its stars and galaxies. The same complexity is reflected on earth in the universal distribution of fractal-like forms, from shorelines to snowflakes. Life brings the level of complexity and uncertainty to an even higher degree. A homogeneous universe, one where the probability for every event is either one or zero, where everything is either exactly the same (say, all hydrogen atoms) or very similar, is a boring universe.

Let's use a game of cards as a model for such a universe. Suppose the rules of this card game are that if you pick an ace from a deck, you win, but if you pick a jack, you lose. All other cards allow you to try again. If the deck is all of one card, the game would be pointless and dull. The probability of winning is either one or zero (depending on what the card is). Let's say we start with all the cards being 9s: the game would go on forever with no winners and no losers. Now we add a single jack. The game becomes more interesting. Then we add one ace. The game is now exciting and even hopeful because each player has the chance of winning as well as losing.

The rules of the card game for our universe would be something more like this: If you draw a king followed by a 4, you get to add three to the next draw, and if you get a numbered card, the probability of getting a chance to draw two cards on the next turn is equal to the numbered card times two if your previous draw was a queen, or three and a half if your previous two draws were both face cards. The rules are so complex that it takes a huge amount of effort to find out what they are.

That is the task of science. To say that the universe and everything in it is complex is to give a description, not a purpose. As a believer in the Creator God, I can understand that the *reason* the universe is complex is to make it interesting to us—and interest suggests the possibility of meaning, free will, love, and connection. As believers, it is our task to explore the complexity of reality in that context of a meaningful universe.

A hot, dense universe of hydrogen atoms is not interesting and of no consequence to anybody. It's like a card game that no one plays because it's so dull. Do such universes exist, perhaps as some of the universes in a hypothetical multiverse? Maybe, but it doesn't matter, because there is no one in that universe to care. A universe like ours but without life is more interesting than a simple monatomic universe, but much less so than ours. And as interesting as life is, consider the enormous leap in meaning that occurred when the first conscious beings emerged.

Now the universe can look at itself, observe itself, and discover that there are limits to how much it can find out about itself. The universe, in the form of humans, can learn many of the rules, but the more we learn, the stranger the game appears to be. And the stranger the game is, the more interesting it is. A universe with conscious life-forms like us has the potential to be of infinite interest to us, and to Whoever was responsible for making sure that the universe is interesting.

Law and Will

God could have chosen to create a perfect world, where all is good, and there is no hardship, no natural disaster, no death. But that would be a *magical* world, not ruled by laws but by constant intervention of the Creator to make things work. This is not to deny that, by the salvation Christ offers us, we humans and all creation eagerly anticipate a world where we experience God's ultimate plan for us (see Paul's words in Rom. 8:18–25). Rather, what I mean is that God chose in His perfect free will to create a universe governed by natural laws. A world where events happen not based on how good they seem to humans but on what can be allowed by those laws. God chose freely to limit His own freedom (as Thomas Oord writes) in this kind of world. God chose a world where $E = mc^2$ and the speed of light is a fixed constant.

He arranged the laws by carefully choosing the constants that go with them to allow for many interesting things to happen: the formation of stars, the creation of the elements, the existence of planets with gravity, and all the wondrous qualities of our own planet. But God also allowed Himself some crucial loopholes, making miracles (events that do not follow natural laws) possible but not the norm. He created life from chemicals, and with life, God produced the natural law of evolution, built into the very first life-forms.

God knew in His omniscience that in this world, living creatures with complex brains would evolve, intelligent enough to be endowed with a soul, and God breathed that soul into them so they could know God. Awareness, consciousness of reality and of God Himself, had come to this universe, and because it is not a magical universe, free will is everywhere. The constraints that God placed upon His own actions apply to us and all creatures as well. God's freedom is reflected in our own freedom.

While we cannot ever predict the path of a single photon or any other particle, it doesn't really matter, since what happens with an individual particle is of very little consequence for the level of reality in which we live. In aggregate, the behavior of a billion particles is easily predictable, and this allows us to formulate laws that consistently work on our scale of existence. The same could be said for individual members of many classes, such as stars, bacteria, jellyfish, and spiders. But it cannot be said for individual humans. Yes, actuaries can tell us how many people in a large population will die at each age, although they cannot predict which people will die. As we cannot predict the behavior of a single gas molecule, we cannot predict the behavior of a single person, though for a different reason. For the molecule, the electron, the photon, and even the bacteria, we cannot predict the future because of the random (stochastic) nature of quantum physics. For us, it is because we have free will.

The actions of individual humans can have incredibly significant effects on the world. Human beings can sometimes act according to well-predicted deterministic pathways. But other times they follow a pathway not found outside of living things: they follow their will. Particles have no will. Neither do other individual members of all other nonliving classes of matter.

Will is something new in the universe. Animals have it to varying degrees, but humans are the champions. The exercise of conscious free will sets the actions of humans, both as individuals and as members of groups, apart from all predictive methods that rely on either deterministic or stochastic models. This is why it is virtually impossible to predict future events when humans are involved.

Around the 1970s, it seemed quite clear to many that the human race was heading for a population crisis. All the math added up to a continuous expansion of growth followed by resource shortages, warfare, and suffering. It didn't happen. The actual population growth turned out to be much less than predicted. There was nothing wrong with the predictions; they were based on good statistics and scientific analysis of current and past data. But they didn't take into account human will. Laws, improved living conditions, and education, all the result of human will, changed the predicted dynamics.

There are those who don't believe in free will. Some think it's because God determines all that happens. Others believe that free will is an illusion, and in fact every decision we make stems from a host of influences and forces that we aren't aware of. I think the evidence for free will is sufficient to say it exists, but the real question is why. It is my contention that free will is absolutely essential and that it is a major factor in God's divine design of the universe. How could creatures without free will bear the image of God, worship Him, and relate to each other as free beings?

The essence of Christian belief is love, and love is only possible when freedom exists. We must choose to love; love cannot be commanded or legislated. We must be free in order to love and to be loved. Free will allows us to have faith and a relationship with God despite the fact that as creatures in His created universe, we can never have conclusive proof of His existence.

Faith and Proof

Many years ago, a postdoctoral fellow working in my laboratory came into my office to tell me that he had found something. He showed me a plastic film on which there were rows of black bands forming a pattern. The pattern had a meaning: it told us about the structure of a particular human gene, and the pattern on this particular film was something new. It had never been seen before, either by us or by anyone else.

At that point I *believed* we had discovered a new form of this gene. But I wasn't sure. We needed to prove it. So we repeated the experiment and got the same result. Then we did it again. Then we checked the sequence of the section of DNA that the gene was in and found exactly the mutation that would explain the new pattern.

We did that three times and got the same result. For each experiment, we also did the same thing to a normal sample and got the expected normal pattern.

We looked at families and found that the new genetic variant was inherited in exactly the way it should be following the known laws of Mendelian genetics.

At that point we had proven that we had found a new genetic variant, thanks to the evidence from several different approaches. I no longer simply *believed* in this genetic variant, I *knew* it was true. We published this result, and several other labs did the same experiments and found the same thing. No one who tried found anything different. The existence of this variant was now a fact, much like the existence of hearts or tectonic plates.

I believe in God. I have evidence for the existence and grandeur of God. Some of this evidence is the historical record of the resurrection of Christ. Peter and Mary Magdalene saw Christ die and met the risen Christ, and thousands of others saw and touched Him also. Their lives were changed. Paul's experience was similar. *Many* saw the direct perceptual evidence, just as many saw my new gene pattern.

But is all of that enough for proof? It could be wrong. There are some people who deny any evidence that comes from the Bible, saying it was all just wishful thinking by followers who exaggerated or misinterpreted the facts, or perhaps a conspiracy to start a new religion. I don't believe them, and I cannot prove them wrong. I am convinced by the evidence for Christ's rising, but not everyone is.

I also have very strong evidence for God that is subjective, related to highly uncertain methods, such as how I feel when I pray, coincidences that I believe are God's way of communicating with me, dreams, and feelings of being in touch with the Holy Spirit. Much of the evidence I have is purely emotional and not verifiable by another observer. I also have some evidence from my own thoughts about the origin of the universe, life, and the human soul, but those are opinions and could well be wrong. To sum it all up, it is a belief, a hypothesis with evidence but not proof.

The next step should be to try to go from these bits of evidence to find proof that my belief is correct, as I did with the new genetic variant, right? Actually, no. I have no interest in doing that. I don't care to get to the point where I can publish the definitive proof that God exists. I am sure to do so is impossible, and even if it were possible, it is not of any interest to me. How can I say this? It seems to go against my scientific training and my certainty that scientific inquiry is the best way to get to know the reality of the natural world.

Like many other human attributes, faith is not subject to scientific methodology. We don't know much about artistic genius, creativity, or even appreciation, but we don't doubt art's existence. I find wonderful beauty and joy in music, but not everyone does. Many people get the same lift from watching ballet. I don't, but I believe them when I see their eyes shine and their mood brighten after a great performance. Perhaps Hebrews 11:3 says it best: "By faith we understand that the universe was created by the word of God, so that what is seen was not made out of things that are visible." I have to admit that when my associate first showed me the new gene pattern on the X-ray film, I felt a chill run down my spine. I wasn't sure, but I did believe we had made a discovery. Every time I go to church, I feel the same thrill of understanding and the joy of a strong belief that I have made a discovery of something true and beautiful. And I am sure of it.

Faith is like musical talent, or an appreciation and understanding of architecture, or even whatever it is that gives us great ideas in physics and helps us solve mathematical theorems. It comes from within us; it is powerful and mysterious and grand. Faith is what takes the place of the experiments that we might think of doing to prove the existence of God. And what faith tells us is that we do not need such proof.

Faith is a powerful force. Some of the most powerful writings I have ever read are the testimonies of people who have undergone great suffering and yet their faith endures. Listen to the speeches of the Rev. Martin Luther King Jr. and so many others who have kept their faith despite oppression, danger, and the harsh reality of their lives. And it is our God-given gift of free will that allows us to choose to have faith and hope. That is why faith can thrive in the face of evil and in the teeth of despair. Even in the darkest hour, the light of faith can shine through and sustain and guide us.

CHAPTER 12

Evolution and Christianity

AFTER I BECAME a Christian, I thought more seriously about evolution because of its controversial nature within Christianity. While most of the material in this chapter played no transformative role in my faith journey, it could play such a part for some readers. Do you, or someone you know, doubt the entire evolution story because of the focus on random, purposeless forces? Do you think that evolutionary theory just doesn't make sense, that something is missing? Or do you think there is no room for God in the evolutionary view of life's diversity? If your answer to any of these is yes, then read on.

What Evolution Is Not

In chapter 5, I explained that evolution does not apply to the origin of life, changes in technology, or any changes outside of biology. Here are four additional statements many people think are true of evolution but actually are not that we should clear up before moving on.

1. Evolution holds that animals change into other animals. Evolution does not say that one animal changes into another (that's what I call

"Pokémon evolution"). Cows always and only give birth to cows, and sheep to sheep, and no sheep ever turned into a cow, just as no monkey or ape ever turned into a human. What evolution describes as the process for change is referred to as common descent (see chapter 5).

2. *Evolution is synonymous with atheism.* Evolution is not atheistic, and it does not require a disbelief in God.

Richard Dawkins said that "Darwin made it possible to be an intellectually fulfilled atheist"—not that Darwin made it *necessary* to be one.[1] Some modern atheists and some modern Christian fundamentalists are in perfect agreement with each other that everyone must choose between God and evolution—you can't have both. This is not true. Biological evolution is accepted by the majority of Catholics, Eastern Orthodox, and mainline Protestant Christians in the United States, as well as by many non-Christian theists.[2]

3. *Neo-Darwinism is the way evolution works.* Neo-Darwinism is not synonymous with evolution. It represents a particular mechanism of variation to allow for evolution. Critics of neo-Darwinism are not attacking the foundation of the theory of evolution.

4. *Mutations are always harmful and cannot provide new genetic information.* I will discuss mutations and other objections to the theory of evolution later.

As I will clarify later in this chapter, this is not to say that there are no problems or issues with evolutionary theory that need to be answered. There are, and answers are being generated all the time. As we will see, some of those answers point not only to the veracity of evolution, but (at least in my mind) to a connection between evolution and a higher power.

Creationist Evolution

The current anti-evolution view, most commonly represented by young-earth creationists, is surprisingly recent, and distinctly American in its origin. It began with a Seventh-day Adventist belief that was formulated in the 1860s and then slowly spread among other Christians. The idea that the earth is only six thousand years old was accepted by very few Christians until the 1961 publication of *The Genesis Flood* by John C. Whitcomb and Henry M. Morris. This book was also the beginning of "creation science," a system of belief that claims to be scientific, although it is actually based on a particular interpretation of the Bible (see chapter 10). The proponents of this worldview sometimes claim that it is the only acceptable view for Christians, and they emphasize that it expressly excludes evolution.

Recently, however, creation scientists at the Institute for Creation Research have somewhat modified their anti-evolution stance. Although they continue to deny that there can be any reconciliation between evolution and a correct reading of the Bible, most creation scientists have come to accept evolution in a limited sense. They have long accepted "microevolution"—evolutionary change wherein a species acquires new and beneficial characteristics based on mutation and natural selection—but they have vehemently argued that the emergence of new species ("macroevolution") from the same process is impossible. However, young-earth creation scientists are now saying that the "kinds" of plants and animals referred to in Genesis were actually a relatively small number. These original kinds then gave rise to all the species alive today through an adaptive process that sounds very much like evolution. The Ark Encounter theme park opened in 2016 by Answers in Genesis even has creative models of what some of the original kinds would have been like. So, a pair of original cat kinds, for example, left the ark and evolved (in six thousand years) into lions, tigers, house cats, jaguars, and so on. This is not only evolution—it would have to be called hyper-evolution, since evolution doesn't work that fast. It is notable, however, that some creationists have come to see some kinds of evolution as required to make sense of the history of God's creation of life on earth.

One difference between the young-earth creationist model for evolution and that of evolutionary biologists (and evolutionary creationists like me) is in the mechanism of variation caused by mutation. For the creationist, all creatures started out genetically perfect (before the fall) and then speciation occurred solely by loss of genetic material. This is in keeping with the view that mutations are always detrimental. The problem is that such a view ignores the realities of mutation.

About Mutations

You might have heard people say that mutations are always harmful, or that all computer engineers know that if you put a random change into a code, the program will likely get worse, not better. This is supposed to show that mutations cannot produce anything worthwhile, and therefore evolution is a bad idea. But that simply is not so. The idea that life began genetically perfect and any subsequent changes, such as mutations, are always harmful and lead to biological degradation does not come from any real science. It comes from a theological view based on a particular biblical interpretation, and it is wrong. The same can be said for the argument that there are so few beneficial mutations that it is not possible for mutations to have any positive effects. Let's look at an example.

If we start with a population of a million cells growing on a dish and add a poison, they will all die. But if we first add a chemical that causes mutations, we find that many of the cells (say, 10 percent) will develop mutations. The majority of those mutations will be harmful, and 90 percent of the mutated cells will die. That leaves ten thousand of the one million total cells in the dish with nonlethal mutations.

Now we add the poison. All the cells with no mutations die. What about the ten thousand mutated cells? Almost all of them die also because their mutations do nothing useful about the poison. But two of those ten thousand cells (0.02%) have a mutation that changes the way the cell transports, metabolizes, or excretes the poison, and those two cells survive. And they reproduce. After a few days, we don't see an empty dish. We see a dish with two visible colonies of healthy, growing cells. Within a week or so, the dish is full of cells that have resisted the poison. This is not a thought experiment; most biologists, including me, have personally done such experiments. There is a good illustration of a similar experiment on a "MEGA plate" from Harvard, available on YouTube.

Yes, this is what some young-earth creationists call "microevolution." The cells are still the same species, but a mutation has overcome enormous odds—in this case, two in a million—and it doesn't matter how rare, unusual, or unlikely such an event is, because biology doesn't care about statistics: all it needs is one success. One in a thousand or (if the population is large enough) one in a billion will do. Statistical arguments just don't work until we get to extremely low probabilities. Saying that something is unlikely has no import in biology.

It is also very important to keep in mind that analogies to software, human information systems, systems engineering, civil engineering, and other nonbiological systems are simply not useful when trying to understand the biological world. While those are wonderful systems that humans can be proud of, they pale to insignificance when we contemplate the wonders of God's amazing creation—life.

Was each new life-form a separate act of creation by God? Or did the progression of the appearance of more and more complex living forms happen according to a natural law of biology, itself created and fashioned by God to work according to His plan? If we approach this subject from a religious viewpoint, I do not see why one explanation is worthier or truer to the faith than the other. In fact, I think the idea of evolution is far more in keeping with the majesty of the Creator than the idea that God needed to separately create all the billions of life-forms (including millions of species of bacteria) that have inhabited our planet.

Design

When we look in detail at the way these hugely diverse life-forms work, we see design. My detailed discussion of how proteins are made in chapter 4 is one of hundreds of examples. Where does this design come from? For many aspects of life, we can understand how the design was created through evolutionary mechanisms. We can see how a specific mutation, gene rearrangement, or change in gene expression led to a new kind of function or structure in an animal or plant. But this is not always true. Sometimes the mechanism that led to the beautiful design of some biological feature seems quite out of reach of our current understanding. Sometimes it simply requires more research, more discoveries of intermediate fossils or the mutational pathways of certain genes, to bring the design process to light.

In recent years, a branch of creation science has "evolved" and has come to be called intelligent design (ID), whose advocates propose that most of evolution, especially those aspects of evolution that involve major biological innovations (such as the development of limbs, wings, and feathers), cannot be explained by the standard Darwinian theory or any other kind of naturalistic evolutionary process. They maintain that the appearance of design in these cases implies a specific creative act by a Creator. There is diversity in the views of different ID proponents (as is the case for evolutionary creationists). Some acknowledge that evolution is likely in many cases, while others are far more convinced that God has stepped in many times to indulge in acts of special creation of life-forms on earth.

One of the objections of ID proponents concerns the evolution of highly complex features they call "irreducibly complex." These features appear to require many intermediary stages in a stepwise evolutionary process and have interactive components that would not have been able to evolve independently. However, the power of natural selection has been demonstrated to allow for the evolution of new structural and functional features, including highly complex ones. Examples of biological systems that appear to be irreducibly complex, such as the eye, the bacterial flagella, the blood-clotting system, and other multicomponent systems, have been shown to arise not all at once (which would require something other than an evolutionary mechanism) but from improvements and the cobbling together of the precursor components from other systems. Once the light-sensitive patches that allowed jellyfish to sense light from dark (and thus hunt more efficiently) had begun to develop into sense organs, evolution was able in incremental steps to render enough improvements to lead to the emergence of an eye. This occurred not once but many separate times in different lineages. Furthermore, it has been found that many of the interactive components of these systems evolved independently for other purposes and were then available for use as a component of the complex system by specific selection-driven modifications.

It is often said that if you find a sandcastle on a beach, it is safe to presume that the structure was designed and built by some form of intelligence, simply because the alternative—that the windblown sand formed a sandcastle by chance—seems to be impossible. Another version of the same argument points out that if you have a junkyard full of parts and a tornado passes by, the chances are zero that the random assortment of junk blown around will result in the construction of a working 747 jet plane. Then there is the analogy with language: if you take a sentence in English and make random changes, you are almost definitely going to make more errors, not create a more meaningful sentence.

These statements are of course all true, but they are all bad analogies for biology. For example, the calculation of the impossibly low probability that a certain protein could have come to exist by chance, considering the gigantic number of possible proteins, may sound valid to a nonbiologist. But no one has ever suggested that proteins arise purely by chance, so the probability calculation is meaningless.

There have been many refutations of the scientific basis of ID from scientists, statisticians, biologists, and physicists, especially when ID proponents argue that conscious willful design, rather than natural selection, drives biological diversity. When applied to the question of the origin of life, scientific refutations have so far been weaker, and the ID argument is stronger.

But I think there is also a theological problem with ID: it makes two assumptions about the nature of God that I believe are contrary to Christian and other religious thought. The first assumption is that the existence of God as Creator of everything is subject to scientific proof within His created universe. I think that assumption is both a theological and scientific fallacy. Intelligent design attempts to prove the Creator by disproving any alternative. But by purporting to prove that life could not evolve without a Creator, the ID movement is digging itself into a God-of-the-gaps hole and forgetting that by His very nature, God is unprovable. Belief in God requires faith, and faith is outside of proof.

My second theological quarrel is with the way ID assumes and thus sees God as designer. If you found a complex watch, you could assume that the maker and designer of the watch was an intelligent human being, and you would be right. But suppose that what you found was a rabbit. A rabbit makes a watch look pretty simple. Certainly, no human, no matter how intelligent, could design a rabbit. I agree that life is designed—but the nature of the design is demeaned by suggesting that it is "intelligent" in the same way a human designer of watches, computers, or aircraft is intelligent. The more we learn about life, the more we understand that the design of life is far more than that. Life was designed by the Creator. It is divine design, not intelligent design, and the mechanisms by which life was designed and created are not currently within our ability to understand.

> I prefer to characterize what we see
> behind the creation of the universe,
> and of life on this planet, as *divine
> design*, not intelligent design.

What we see on this planet is a beautiful diversity of life, all of it clearly designed to perform at a peak of function. When we consider the miraculous, majestic processes that govern how life evolves without any need for a creative act for each separate species of beetle or termite, we can only sink to our knees in worship at the glory of the Creator of life and all of its processes. This is why I prefer to characterize what we see behind the creation of the universe, and of life on this planet, as *divine design*, not intelligent design.

A Historical Perspective on Evolutionary Theory

While intelligent design does not succeed in proving the existence of a supernatural Designer, some of their challenges to evolutionary theory are becoming increasingly valid and have led to productive research on how evolution works. This research has resulted in new approaches and concepts of evolutionary theory, which, to my mind, are more consonant with a Christian point of view than the traditional theory. Before going into more detail about these new ideas, we should take a closer look at the history of evolutionary thought up to now.

When we covered the basics of evolution in chapter 5, we saw how natural selection chooses from individual variants those that are likely to survive and reproduce. But where do these variants come from? Darwin had no idea. In *On the Origin of Species*, Darwin states "I have hitherto sometimes spoken as if the variations . . . were due to chance. This, of course, is a wholly incorrect expression, but it serves to acknowledge plainly our ignorance of the cause of each particular variation."[3] The idea that such variants arose by random mutations entered the standard evolutionary theory much later.

At the beginning of the twentieth century, it was known that bacteria could survive stresses like loss of a particular food supply or exposure to drugs by mutating certain genes that changed their phenotype. What was not known yet was whether this meant that the organism changed deliberately and purposefully to respond to the situation. The alternative was that lots of different mutations occurred by chance in different individuals, and if one of them had a positive effect (such as allowing for metabolism of a different food source), it was selected for, and the individual with that particular mutation survived and prospered.

The results of experiments done in the 1940s indicated that mutations occurred randomly in the population, and then they were selected for their relative fitness. This was the origin of the idea that evolution was blind, without purpose or direction. Further research throughout the second half of the twentieth century led to an explosion of knowledge in cellular and molecular biology, including genetics and how DNA functions and mutates. The combination of molecular genetics with the more traditional evolutionary biological study of fossils and phylogenetics resulted in what is known as the "modern synthesis" theory of evolution.

The modern synthesis, sometimes called neo-Darwinism or the neo-Darwinian modern synthesis (NDMS), includes the idea that genes and their variants are the fundamental units of evolution. Over time, other, less firmly established principles, some of which are more philosophical than scientific, were incorporated into the thinking of some scholars. Among these are gradualism— the idea first proposed by Darwin that *all* evolutionary change is slow and proceeds by small, stepwise changes, each of which is selectively advantageous. Eventually, over millions of years, these small changes then add up to the enormous differences we see today between species and orders.

Many of the neo-Darwinians also emphasize the random nature of mutations and conclude that evolution (and biology in general) is a blind, accidental process, with no particular direction or purpose. I will discuss this in more detail shortly.

Another tenet of the neo-Darwinian modern synthesis is the concept of adaptationism. This is the idea that all evolutionary change is directly due to some kind of adaptation of organisms to their environment. While this seems to be logically consistent with the powerful engine of natural selection in shaping species, some evolutionary biologists like Ernst Mayr and Stephen Jay Gould have pointed out that the evidence from the fossil record is not always supportive of adaptationism. Furthermore, the neutral theory of Motoo Kimura, which does not include universal adaptation, has been shown to be valid. According to this theory, a great deal (perhaps most) of evolutionary change is due to nonadaptive (neutral) genetic drift. Isolated small populations can diverge genetically due to chance differences in allele frequencies that have nothing to do with adaptation or selection.

The NDMS withstood the findings of neutral genetic drift, punctuated equilibrium (see chapter 5), and other exceptions and challenges to the doctrine of random mutation as the key producer of biological variation. But recently, many scientists have begun to argue that the NDMS has become outdated. Creationists and intelligent design critics of evolution have a point when they claim that the NDMS cannot sufficiently account for some of the major shifts in biological features during the history of life on earth.

The NDMS is characterized by a strongly gene-centered approach, perfectly expressed by Richard Dawkins in his book *The Selfish Gene.* According to this view, the bodies of creatures are simply vehicles for the true masters of biology—the replicating genes—because it is genes that are selected for in evolution, not individuals (phenotypes), which are merely carrying out the instructions of the genes. This idea has been challenged by the recognition that the complexity of life extends to the level of the physiology of the cell and its environment as they interact with the genome. There have been new insights from many directions that suggest that this gene-centered emphasis is too narrow to explain all the sources of genetic variation that can cause groups of animals to diverge. One of the leaders of the anti-gene-centered movement in evolution is British physiologist Denis Noble, whose book *Dance to the Tune of Life* has provided a great deal of evidence to dispute the claim that genes are the center of evolution as well as biology.

To quote Denis Alexander on a similar note: "The 'selfish gene' had its day in the sun, but has now been replaced by the image of a finely tuned genomic system in which each type of gene product cooperates via an intricate networking complex to generate the music of life. The vast array of epigenetic signals whereby genes are switched on or off ensures a steady flow of two-way communication between the genome and its wider environments."[4]

The Extended Evolutionary Synthesis

Some evolutionary biologists have put forward a number of ideas that directly challenge the established NDMS with new ways of thinking about how evolution works. The collection of these ideas is often referred to as the extended evolutionary synthesis (EES). They include niche construction, which is a novel view of how organisms carry on a two-way interaction with their environment. These interactions are dynamic and nonrandom, and they include examples such as beavers building dams, corals building islands, and humans doing just about everything we do. Another important part of the EES is developmental evolution (evo devo), which studies the effects of developmental genes (the genes that determine the initial growth of an organism—as an embryo, for example) on evolutionary patterns. We have recently learned that there is an entire category of genes whose function it is to control the expression of other genes, both during development and in later life. The complexity of these gene-regulatory networks is still in the process of being understood, but there seems to be no question that these networks must have an important role in evolution. For further information on the EES from a Christian perspective, please see my paper in *Perspectives on Science and Christian Faith*.[5]

Another exciting area of research concerns the origin of innovation in evolution. Andreas Wagner, author of the book *Arrival of the Fittest*, has come up with a fascinating hypothesis. Wagner's group found, both in laboratory experiments and using computer models, that there is not just one way to build a protein with a particular function—there are millions of ways to do it. When they made single mutations to a protein, changing only one amino acid, they found that a large fraction of these mutants produced the same phenotype as the original sequence. This is called robustness, and it is a key feature of all biological systems. And, it turns out, this same robustness allows for innovation because after many neutral mutational steps, just one more change can produce a protein with a brand-new, useful function. The Wagner group found that the same was true for regulatory networks and metabolic pathways.

It must be noted that the exciting and innovative ideas of the EES do not contradict or demolish the modern synthesis. They simply expand and extend the known mechanisms of evolutionary biology into new fields of research, much like modern physics extended classical Newtonian physics to the world of the very small.

Convergence and Constraints in Evolution

Although not technically part of the EES, the phenomenon of convergence is also an important area of research that is changing the way we think about evolution. Evolutionary convergence refers to the findings that similar features are often found in organisms that are not related by direct common ancestry. For example, wings developed independently in insects, birds, and mammals (bats). Simon Conway Morris's book *Life's Solution: Inevitable Humans in a Lonely Universe* documents hundreds of such examples throughout the various realms of life. The camera eye, found in mammals and invertebrates like octopi, had to arise through separate evolutionary mechanisms and was not inherited from a common ancestor. The same is true for traits like echolocation, fins, and even intelligence.

One implication of convergence is that there are constraints to what evolution can do. Gould famously said that if we were to "wind back the tape of life" and let it play again, "the chance becomes vanishingly small" that we would get the same results from evolution, including human intelligence.[6] This statement was based on his idea (generally accepted by biologists at the time) that evolution follows no particular rules other than natural selection choosing from an unconstrained set of random or accidental variations. But convergence and the existence of constraints imply that that isn't true. Evolution cannot accomplish all things. For example, while many creatures fly, none of them use jet propulsion and fixed wings (though some organisms have developed jet propulsion for swimming); instead, they all use flapping wings to produce lift. Convergence also suggests that many biological features (like wings and eyes) are inevitable, since they have arisen so many times independently, and the different versions have many features in common, even at the molecular and biochemical levels. This characteristic of inevitability also suggests that evolution has a direction, and that if we were able to rewind the tape (or found primitive life on another planet), we would indeed be able to predict a great deal of what would happen with time.

The Theology of Evolution

It is a deeply religious idea that God endowed a primitive cell with the power not only of life, not only to reproduce itself, but to change, to give rise slowly and inevitably to new forms, which gradually and with great wonder led to us. What makes this all so wonderful is the simple yet elegant form of the basic law of biology that allows and *requires* evolution to occur—natural selection. I view natural selection as the greatest gift of God to the planet. The power of natural selection is that it can create complexity from simplicity, and it can lead to the occurrence of extremely unlikely events. It has a godlike power precisely because it came from God. Natural selection and belief in God are not only noncontradictory but they are inextricably linked and harmonious.

The role of chance and accident should never be eliminated from any biological theory. But it's important to remember that what we see as chance or random events might appear that way to us because we don't know *everything*, and—like with the coin or card tossing

I discussed in chapter 2—we can't formulate equations and laws to account for chance in biology. If we were godlike, maybe we could gain such understanding. In other words, it's possible that what we see as chance God sees as natural law.

> Natural selection and belief in God are not only noncontradictory but they are inextricably linked and harmonious.

If evolutionary progress is real, and if convergence is indeed a sign of patterns of evolutionary constraint that suggest pathways for life to follow, then even if we aren't clear on what (or Who) the driver for purpose is, aren't the data themselves pointing to teleology as a distinct possibility? When a very subtle, minor change in the timing of gene expression during development can be amplified to the point of leading to an entirely different body shape, how can we be sure such alterations are entirely random? Once we remove the limitations of looking only at random point mutations in structural genes and expand our view to include a great deal more of the genomic territory, as well as additional mechanisms including epigenetics, can we say that we have also greatly expanded the opportunities for divine intervention in the evolutionary process? What do all of the new data and concepts tell us about the potential for God's role in evolution?

While the scientists doing research on the EES are not necessarily believers, their work seems to me to have strong implications for Christian faith. The theological implications of any form of the EES are complex and broad. The extended theory of evolution does not see chance as the *only* driving force for evolutionary variation or hold that *everything* came about due to natural selection.

It recognizes the overwhelming complexity of biological systems and the limited value of trying to reduce any aspect of biology to a simple reductionist theory. Perhaps at some point in the future, the EES, convergence, or some other novel evolutionary theory will lead to new pointers to the majesty of God's creative design for life.

Evolutionary Creation

I consider myself to be an evolutionary creationist (see chapter 5). An elevator speech description of my belief might go something like this: "I am a Christian who believes in the Apostles' Creed, including the incarnation and resurrection of Christ, who was wholly man and wholly God. At the same time, I accept evolution as the best explanation for the diversity of life on earth, and I fully accept empirical mainstream science as the best way to understand all natural phenomena. If you want to know more details, we will need to continue this conversation once this elevator reaches the ground floor."

The evolutionary creationist worldview is most ably presented by the organization founded by Francis Collins: BioLogos. Here are some extracts from their website that provide the best description of the evolutionary creation (EC), or theistic evolution (TE) view.

> We believe that God also reveals himself in and through the natural world he created, which displays his glory, eternal power, and divine nature. Properly interpreted, Scripture and nature are complementary and faithful witnesses to their common Author. . . .
>
> We believe in the historical incarnation of Jesus Christ as fully God and fully man. We believe in the historical death and resurrection of Jesus Christ, by which we are saved and reconciled to God. . . .
>
> We believe that God typically sustains the world using

faithful, consistent processes that humans describe as "natural laws." Yet we also affirm that God works outside of natural law in supernatural events, including the miracles described in Scripture. . . .

We reject ideologies such as Materialism and Scientism that claim science is the sole source of knowledge and truth. . . .

We believe that God created humans in biological continuity with all life on earth, but also as spiritual beings. God established a unique relationship with humanity by endowing us with his image and calling us to an elevated position within the created order.[7]

In other words, evolutionary creationism retains every part of the basic Christian faith. Evolutionary creationists generally accept mainstream science but reject scientism, and they accept the existence of miracles and the supernatural under the aegis of God.

This point of view has been controversial both for some Christians and for atheistic philosophers and scientists who find the bridge between faith and science to be illusory, but I think the evolutionary creationist view represents the future of Christianity. It is supported by a large number of Christian denominations (including the Roman Catholic Church).[8]

The theological view of evolutionary creationism does not assert specific details about how evolution and God's sustaining care for the world can be viewed in a Christian context. Evolutionary creationists may hold to various beliefs about the intersection of scientific evolution and the creative power of God's will.

Providential Evolution

I have recently considered a new way to think about the connections between evolutionary science and Christianity that I call "providential evolution." The idea of providential evolution is a strictly theological one and is not meant to replace or modify the scientific understanding of evolution as the foundation for biological science.

Many atheistic evolutionists acknowledge that evolution has a direction and stop there. But what, or Who, directs it? An atheist can argue that no director is needed other than natural selection. For me, evolution makes God's providence in the biological world apparent. I believe that the direction of evolution toward greater complexity—including multicellularity, efficient energy conversion, the vertebrate body plan, the development of neural circuitry, and the emergence of brains—all have a purpose determined by God's will. In ways that we cannot understand, it is God's providence that exercises that will on the biological world, much as His providence answers our prayers and allowed the miracles of His own incarnation and resurrection on earth.

Providential evolution should reassure both the Christian believer and the agnostic that evolution is not only consistent with but is also a fundamental part of God's work. God granted humans a soul, and we are created in His image. But the soul must inhabit a body, and the human body was created by God using providential evolution.

While some evolutionary biologists like Gould argued that evolution lacks any purpose or direction, there is no evidence for this. In a paper published in the journal *Perspectives on Science and Christian Faith*, I argue that there is scientific evidence for purpose in biology and evolution and that teleology is built into the basic mechanism of how evolution works: "[T]he roots of biological teleology do not lie in the *action* of evolutionary processes. Instead, I believe they can be found in the very *fabric* of the evolutionary process. In other words, purpose is built into the central, deepest biochemical meaning of what evolution is."[9]

Faith and Scripture tell us that God plays an active role in biology as well as in the rest of creation. While scientific confirmation is neither necessary nor possible, it is valuable to seek harmony between the two books of God's revelation to humanity, the Book of Words and the Book of Works. I find confirmation of the enormous beauty and intricacy of the living world reflected in the new theories of biological evolution. It is possible that such approaches, besides being scientifically defensible, may also lead (as has almost every line of research into biology so far) to surprising and even spiritually informative conclusions about how the Creator did His work, and why.

Evolutionary Creation in My Journey to Faith

When, with a great deal of struggle to overcome my long history as an anti-theistic atheist, I was finally able to admit that Christ's call to me had gotten through, I allowed the joy of salvation to overcome and overwhelm my liberated soul. I spent quite some time on an emotional roller coaster as the scales fell from my eyes, and I began to see and feel the amazing grace of God's love. But there was a problem.

I was an active scientific researcher, and I didn't know a single other scientist who was a professing Christian. I didn't even know *of* any such scientist. I had heard of creation science and, like all my peers, rejected it. I knew that there were wonderful theologians who also said that science and Christian faith could be compatible. But all actual scientists (I thought) were either atheists or agnostics, or if they did profess some religion, I saw no sign in them of the intensity that was gripping me. I felt completely alone.

And then I found *The Language of God: A Scientist Presents Evidence for Belief.* I knew who Francis Collins was, of course, and I had even met him at a small symposium on genetics and ethics, but I had had no idea that he was a Christian. Reading his book was electrifying—I must have shouted "Yes!" a hundred times to an empty room. I was not alone after all, praise God!

The Language of God is a landmark book that describes how it is possible to be an ardent Christian who accepts evolution. Other wonderful books have helped thousands of people hold on to their precious faith while accepting the modern world of science, including evolution. These books include Denis Lamoureux's *I Love Jesus and I Accept Evolution*, Karl Giberson's *Saving Darwin*, Darrel Falk's *Coming to Peace with Science*, and Deborah and Loren Haarsma's *Origins*.

I began to participate in discussions on the BioLogos website, went to a meeting of the American Scientific Affiliation, and found that besides Francis and me, there were thousands of scientists who were active, dedicated Christians and had no difficulty reconciling their faith with good science. I met many of these people; some became my friends, and some are now well-known as authors of books or participants in discussions and debates. Some of these people had previously been young-earth creationists, others had been atheists or agnostics. All of them had seen a light and were called to lift up the lamp of Christian faith through evolutionary creationism so that it could shine into the souls of the lost like me.

Students who were on the verge of rejecting Christianity, who felt forced to choose between their faith and the science they were learning in college, have found a third way, a way to see that you _can be a Christian and a scientist_. Pastors, struggling to keep their congregations aware—but not afraid—of the blows from secular society that use science as a weapon to create doubt, have come to see with renewed vigor the compatibility of Christian faith with the reality of science. Youth leaders, church lay leaders, and seminary students have seen the value of the evolutionary creationist message. Agnostics and people of spiritual yearnings who had shunned Christianity because of fears of being trapped in an anti-scientific worldview have found in evolutionary creationism the path to allow the joy of God's grace to fill their souls without any sacrifice of their reason.

Evolutionary creationism does not have all the answers, and on some points, there is a diversity of opinions. I think it is fitting and just for us to argue, to disagree, to develop ideas. There are answers to all our questions, answers known to God, slowly revealed to us human mortals through His two great books. There is a lot we don't know. We don't know if the newer evolutionary theories are correct. We don't know if life originated on some other planet, if the galaxy is full of other Christ worshippers, or if we are all there is. We don't know how and how much God intervenes in any part of our lives or in His creation. But we do know that we live in a world lovingly created by God, and we are made in His image.

The task of Christian scientists like me is twofold: to continue the hard work of learning from Scripture and from nature all we can about God and our place in His creation, and to ensure that the faith endures, stays strong, and allows and encourages all who seek truth to gain the same peace, joy, and love that I finally found in my long journey.

CHAPTER 13

Science and Faith Together

The first gulp from the glass of science will turn
you into an atheist, but at the bottom of the glass
God is waiting for you.
        —Werner Heisenberg

WHILE THERE IS some question as to whether Werner Heisenberg actually said those words,[1] I think the sentiment conveyed is accurate. Heisenberg did write the following: "I have repeatedly been compelled to ponder on the relationship of these two regions of thought [science and religion], for I have never been able to doubt the reality of that to which they point."[2] These quotes are quite germane to my own experience. As I have also heard from other experienced scientists, the deeper one delves into the intricate scientific details of nature, the more evidence can be found for faith in God.

I have told the long story of my journey to faith, but we're not quite at the end. Once I had accepted Jesus Christ as my Savior and felt that my purpose in life was to serve God, how did I proceed as a scientist? And what have I learned since then about my faith and its relation to science?

The first question I had to ask myself when I fully understood that I believed in God and accepted Jesus Christ as my Savior was this: Can a scientist who holds a fully scientific worldview also believe in God without going crazy from the "culture war" between the two?

Before answering that question from my own perspective, let's take a look at it through a historical lens.

Some Historical Context

After the collapse of the Roman Empire, Europe and the Mediterranean world entered a period of economic, cultural, and technological regression that lasted about half a millennium. During this era, people believed—as they did in other cultures around the world— that the best and only true answers to questions about the reality of existence came from ancient authority. The sources could be verbal or written historical, religious, or philosophical texts. Whether it was the Gospels, the Old Testament, the Quran, the Upanishads, the writings of the ancient classical philosophers, or an oral tradition of knowledge, answers to everything one might want to know were to be found in (and only in) ancient wisdom. In Europe, the few people with any education at all were members of the clergy. Wisdom, knowledge, and religion were intricately bound together. Truth about every aspect of the world was synonymous with God's truth. There simply was no secular alternative to the knowledge stored in holy books.

The rediscovery of classical works of science, art, literature, and poetry that heralded the Renaissance brought new light and a flourishing of artistic and intellectual life, but initially also reinforced the belief that knowledge and wisdom came from the past. The revolutionary idea that new information about the world could be discovered by new observations or experiments appeared in the work of Franciscan friar Roger Bacon in thirteenth-century England, and "natural philosophy" slowly gained respect in medieval universities. But it was in the seventeenth century that what we now know as the scientific revolution took off. Modern science (initially still referred to as natural philosophy) started to take shape thanks to the efforts of brilliant pioneers such as Francis Bacon, Copernicus, Newton, Galileo, Cunitz, Hooke, Kepler, and others. The concept that *new knowledge* could be generated began to take hold as global exploration and economic progress led to an era of openness of thought. Experimental science, a truly novel concept at the time, began to make inroads into the realm of knowledge that had been exclusively owned by religion. Newton published his ideas on how things move, fall, and interact. The church yielded slowly and cautiously at first, and then with more of a sense of collaboration. The age of the Enlightenment had dawned.

> Scientists tended to be as religious
> as everyone else, and most thought of
> themselves as working to uncover the
> glorious truth of God's majestic creation.

Those making scientific observations and performing experiments were discovering wonders about the way the world works, and these discoveries were far from being anti-religious. On the contrary, many saw them as confirmatory of the glory and majesty of God's creation. By the nineteenth century, it had become clear to farsighted clerics in all the major religions that physical science was not an implicit enemy of religion. Scientists tended to be as religious as everyone else, and most thought of themselves as working to uncover the glorious truth of God's majestic creation. Most of the new scientific ideas from the great age of science that blossomed in the eighteenth and nineteenth centuries were in fact more in harmony with religious beliefs than some of the views they replaced.

The Origins of Biology as a Science

As science continued to make progress, there was a tacit understanding that the realm of science was physics and the realm of theology was metaphysics. The definitions of those two realms were different than they are today. For example, the nature and origin of life was not considered to be a subject suitable for science. Life—and human life, specifically—was still a completely mysterious subject, not easily approachable by the methods of science. On the other hand, discoveries in chemistry, research on thermodynamics, and the intricate mechanical inventions of the time provoked nothing but admiration and respect from everyone, clergy included.

We know that when Darwin began his work, biology had already been divided along lines of orthodoxy. Some felt that all work in biology had to conform to Scripture, since life was squarely within the realm of the metaphysical, or divine, magisterium. Others, such as most of Darwin's friends and teachers, held the view that biology could become a science much like chemistry and the physics of motion. This meant that the rules of science, as articulated by Francis Bacon, would apply to scientific inquiries on the nature and detailed mechanisms of life.

These thinkers dared to suggest that the scientific method that was immensely successful for the study of the nature of gases and the projectile vectors of cannonballs could be followed for biology. This was not an anti-religious movement—it was simply a group of philosophers (many of them clergymen) who wanted to move the dividing line between physics and metaphysics so that life and all things living now fit into the scientific category. They did not, of course, include perception, consciousness, human emotion, social interactions—aspects of life that we would now study under social science or psychology. Linnaeus, Lamarck, and others began this trend where it needed to begin, with classification schemes of living beings. There could be little objection to the idea of classifying all the creatures of the earth, sea, and sky according to their physical nature, shape, and function.

However, some clerics were annoyed by any incursion by the forces of objective science into the forbidden territory of the divine nature of life. In 1828, the chemical synthesis of urea, a simple molecule found in all living creatures, had created a firestorm of controversy. It had been widely held until then that all substances from living beings had special properties, including a mysterious "vital force," that could not exist outside of living things.

The fact that urea could be made in a laboratory was the first blow against the exclusion of biology from the realm of objective research. But vitalism was able to adapt to the new discoveries by shifting its emphasis from the specific chemicals found in life to the special "something" that made life alive and more than just a collection of chemicals.

It was generally agreed that life had this metaphysical quality. This seemed to be confirmed by the fact that simply mixing together all the chemicals found in even the simplest organism would not lead to spontaneous generation of a living organism. Abbot Lazzaro Spallanzani, a clergyman and scientific pioneer, showed that the spontaneous generation of life was not possible. He believed that his research was also a powerful proof of the transcendent nature of life—life that could not arise from nonlife in a dish of rotten meat or an infusion of organic matter.

At the beginning of the twentieth century, biology was still a very young and shaky science, but it had become a real science. No one today would think of going to their priest or minister with a question about the circulation of blood or the health consequences of eating a particular diet. During the course of the twentieth century, major breakthroughs such as the discovery of the genetic code, the molecular biology of the cell, and so many advances in ecology, physiology, and evolutionary biology have put biology on an equal footing with chemistry and physics. The applications of biological research have been profound for human health and well-being. Medicine continues to make great strides using the biological discoveries of basic research in cell biology, biochemistry, and biophysics.

> The human pursuit of scientific truth
> about the universe is a magnificent
> activity of worshipful praise and acclaim
> for the glory of God's creation.

The enormous historical success of science in all fields has led to a crisis of faith for millions of people. What are they to believe when science seems to make God irrelevant? This question assumes that science and God are two alternative, mutually exclusive answers to the questions of reality. I think that is a myth. I came to see God as real because of my scientific training, not in spite of it, and what I believe in is a synthesis of science and faith.

Credo (What I Believe)

What does this synthesis look like? I believe that God is the Creator of the universe and all it contains. I believe that the human pursuit of scientific truth about the universe is a magnificent activity of worshipful praise and acclaim for the glory of God's creation. We human beings were meant to understand and reveal all the wonder and majesty of God's creative acts. There cannot be any contradiction between the ideas of science and the Word of God. If such a contradiction appears to exist, then we have made an error, either in our science or in our theology, or in both.

I have found that faith in God is completely consistent with a scientific understanding of nature. I would go further and say that a belief in the power and value of a scientific worldview is actually an important ingredient in a strong faith in God the Creator. That means that there is not, and there cannot be, any contradiction between any scientific statement and any statement of faith. I am aware that this sentiment goes against the current trend of dividing the human population into believers in God and believers in science, a false dichotomy that has been loudly proclaimed by extremists on both sides of a phony "war." Many other voices have also been raised against this falsehood, and many wonderful books (listed in appendix B) have been written to deny the necessity of such a division in how people think about the nature of reality.

When I first became aware that I was a believer, I wondered what effect it would have on my scientific worldview. I was quite delighted to find that, if anything, my scientific worldview was strengthened. Worship of God has led me to want to probe deeper into the truth about the universe. Faith in God is a wonderful asset to a scientist who strives to understand the meaning behind the laws of physics and biology that rule our universe.

My religious beliefs include the following: God created the universe and all the laws of physics, the forces of nature, and the mathematical constants that govern the matter and energy of the universe. God created life on earth, and with it the laws related to how living creatures function, reproduce, and evolve. Among these God-given laws is the evolution of millions of distinct species by natural selection. God created the body of humans from "the dust of the earth," through His law of evolution by natural selection and then gave them the divine gift of a soul ("breathing life into his nostrils"). None of these creation events are contradicted by scientific findings.

Including concepts of a divine creation in my science-based worldview gives me a profoundly more sophisticated viewpoint than I had when I was an atheist. It opens new questions, suggests new and wonderful possibilities, reawakens my thirst for knowledge, and invigorates my sense of wonder at the beauty of life and the universe.

Knowledge about the universe is a God-given gift, and science is the tool that humans use to understand the truth of the creation. Adam, the first true man, gave names to things: classification is one of the first required steps in understanding nature. But scientific experimentation, hypothesis generation, theoretical model building, and all the tools of science are not the only ways to experience and understand truth. If they were, then all the nonscientists in the world (most of humanity) would be ignorant fools. And I know that isn't true. I have friends who are painters, musicians, poets, and philosophers, and they too teach me undeniable truths about reality.

There is an erroneous idea that while scientists are always open-minded and searching for new ways to see truth, people of faith think they have it all figured out—they believe they know the final truth, the *dogma* that cannot change. In reality, open-minded people are open-minded about science *and* faith, and close-minded people are dogmatic about both.

Magic, Mystery, and Natural Law

There is a fundamental concept that science and Christianity hold in common: the belief that the world we know is governed by natural law. This should not be taken for granted because it is a relatively new idea in human history. Early pagan religions and philosophical systems were not based on law but on magic, the whims of gods and demigods, and (later) on logic. Logic seems to be a rational way of thinking and therefore closely related to science, but it is not science. Of course, logic is a reason-based approach to view reality, and it is a critical part of the way science is done, but it is quite a different thing from scientific law. We now know that there are scientific laws and truths about the universe that, contrary to the ideas of Aristotle and his associates, cannot always be grasped by the application of logic. Natural law cannot be derived logically—it has to be discovered through observation of and experimentation with the natural world as it is. Because of this commitment to law, both Christianity and modern science had to reject the Aristotelian system of truth as firmly as they rejected magic and the capricious will of untold numbers of demigods and demons.

The importance of natural law in Christianity is evidenced by the early scientists, many of whom were fervent Christians. People like Isaac Newton, Michael Faraday, Maria Cunitz, and Robert Boyle were convinced that their work in discovering the fundamental laws of nature were divinely blessed efforts.

Before the advent of science, proof of anything was hard to come by. Abraham, Moses, John the Baptist, and Paul the apostle all had personal experiences of the reality of God, and they used these experiences to convince many of the reality of God's might and goodness. Many, but not all. Those who saw Moses come down from the mountain were free to not believe his message. Not everyone who heard the Gospel from the apostles chose to follow Christ. Not even everyone who witnessed Jesus Himself became a believer.

The emergence of science changed things. It was a new way of gaining knowledge and, more importantly, a level of certainty. Of course, science is rarely certain about most things it studies, and even when it appears certain, there is always the possibility that the picture is not complete. But, despite that, the method of science has given humankind an unprecedented tool to gain certainty, and there are many who believe that with this method *all truth* can be distinguished from all falsehood. They think that the tool of science can turn everything that is uncertain into certain knowledge. This includes the many questions we now have about the nature of the human being and the mind, the meaning of consciousness, the existence of a soul, the nature of art and beauty, the enigma of morality and altruism, and even good and evil. If this seems like a reflection of Adam's original sin, it isn't a coincidence.

Faith and Science

When I contemplate the science-faith relationship, I tend to see many more similarities between the two than common modern perceptions acknowledge. Religious mysticism teaches that we may study and perhaps even understand certain aspects of God, although to accomplish this requires years of training, hard work, meditation, and spiritual enlightenment. However, there are aspects of God that are simply beyond what humans can even approach. Similarly, a research scientist struggling to understand a part of the universe (for example, how stars are formed or how genes are regulated) must spend years in training and then in hard work, using imagination, creativity, and technical expertise. But, as we now know, there are profound and rational arguments to be made that a complete knowledge of the workings of the universe is theoretically impossible.

The true religious mystic and the true scientist are humble before the immense majesty of God or the universe. Each knows that for human beings there are limits beyond which no one may go. Yet each is consumed by a longing that is deep and profound. The mystic desires to cleave his soul to God. The scientist does not speak in such personal terms, but what she seeks is to feel her mind in tune with a beautiful truth. I submit that an objective observer would not be able to distinguish the mystic in his meditative union with God from the scientist in her moment of discovery.

Both Christianity and modern science allow the existence of

mystery—in other words, they both allow the possibility of questions that cannot be answered. Some materialists might deny this in the case of science, and it is true that most early scientists would have argued that science strove to answer all questions about the natural world and did not accept the existence of mystery. Many would argue the same today. They would claim that just because we don't know the answer to a question, it doesn't mean we will never know it.

But as we have seen, there are a number of questions that science has *proven* cannot be answered. When a scientist says that a question cannot be answered, what that means is, "It's a mystery that cannot be solved. So don't ask." There are many such mysteries, and their nature might not be all that different from the mystery of the Trinity or the resurrection.

A Simulated Universe?

A very good illustration of the similarity between scientific and religious mysteries was recently brought home to me by a panel discussion led by the astronomer Neil deGrasse Tyson on the question of whether we live in a real or a simulated universe. According to the simulation hypothesis, we are characters in a much more advanced analogy of a computer game, something akin to the fictional world of the film *The Matrix*. As the argument goes, if we lesser mortals can simulate reality at some level, then some putative highly intelligent aliens must have already become incredibly good at simulations, and we could very well be living in one of their projects.

Apparently, this hypothesis is being taken seriously by some scientists. My question is: If you are going to talk about simulators (those who made the simulations), how exactly is that different from talking about a Creator? Why is the idea of a simulated universe acceptable for scientific discussion while the idea of a universe created and maintained by God is not?

The consensus, if there was any, seemed to be that if we *are* a simulation—in other words, created—then there should be clues to that in the rules by which we are playing the game, better known as the laws of physics. In fact, one of the panelists, theoretical physicist S. James Gates Jr., said that he has found evidence of error-correcting codes in some of the equations of symmetry related to string theory. This appears to be evidence that the universe was computed rather than a random outcome of accidental causes.

It certainly does seem that we are living in a mathematical universe, according to Max Tegmark, another physicist, who wrote a book on the subject. Many theists have pointed out that the physical laws that govern everything are generally simple and elegant mathematical formulas, and that this is just what one would expect in a universe created by a being. The setting of the physical constants (chapter 3) is also consistent with some super-intelligent game designer far, far away.

I find that the more we learn about the nature of reality and think scientifically about how the world works, the more we see the hand of a Creator God. The only step that is missing in the thought processes of some atheists appears to be making the leap from the possibility that we are all here thanks to the creative work of a sixteen-year-old, super-smart alien sitting in his basement and creating simulated universes on his laptop to the idea that we are all here thanks to the creation of a God who is omnipotent, omniscient, and good.

A Caution About Science and Faith

While I have been stressing the connections between science and faith, we must be careful in our drive to see how science and theology point to one single truth to avoid making the mistake of allowing one to unduly influence our understanding of the other. We cannot improve our understanding of Scripture by artificially inserting sciency-sounding material into our worldview, nor can we (as the creation scientists do) get a grasp on scientific truth by checking it against Scripture. Since the Book of Words (Scripture) and the Book of Works (nature) are written by the same Author, we must have faith that the best science, arrived at by purely scientific methods, and the best theology, arrived at by study and analysis of Scripture, will in the end meet at one single point of perfect harmony.

> We must have faith that the best science,
> arrived at by purely scientific methods, and
> the best theology, arrived at by study and
> analysis of Scripture, will in the end meet
> at one single point of perfect harmony.

We have a long way to go to get there. One of the stumbling blocks on this path is the deliberate distortion of both science and Christian theology by those with agendas that have little to do with good science or good theology. I have seen people (most of them not actually scientists) claim that "science tells us" things that are in fact speculative, not well established, and sometimes quite wrong.

There is often a hidden anti-religious agenda behind the speculations, inferences, hypotheses, and subjective interpretations that some are promoting to the public as established scientific truth. In the long run, such behavior is bound to be counterproductive, because it is absolutely true that in science the truth will always eventually come out.

Some of the pseudoscientific ideas that have found their way into popular consciousness are purported (mostly by militant atheists) to support atheism and to present problems for Christian faith. A good example is the idea that life must exist on other planets. In fact, most Christians I have discussed this with, including several Christian astronomers and astrobiologists, see no reason why Christians would have any difficulty with extraterrestrial life. I happen to be skeptical about this for scientific reasons, but theologically, alien life would do nothing to shake my faith in God. Glib pronouncements of evolutionary mechanisms for explaining all aspects of human nature, along with the claim that science has found that human beings are nowhere as special as we like to think, are not scientific but philosophical statements. Other pseudoscientific claims that have become popular is that DNA is not a code, that we understand how a universe can spontaneously arise from nothing, and that the origin of life is now almost completely understood and explained by chemical evolution. None of these are true. Theologians, pastors, and Christian laypeople should be advised that they might not be dealing with legitimate science every time they hear somebody (scientist or not) claim that "science says" something, and they should be cautious about trying to incorporate such philosophical views into Christian theological thinking.

All Natural Law Comes from God

Any phenomenon—lightning, photosynthesis, human friendship— might be described by a religious person as being so wonderful, so mysterious, so amazing that it must come from God. An atheist might say, "No, actually there is a simple, natural explanation that does not require the existence of a God."

Yes, there is always a natural explanation, which in no way rules out the transcendent idea of divine agency. I believe in God based on what we know about the natural world, not on what we don't know. God does not fill gaps of as yet unrevealed knowledge. God is responsible for all knowledge, and for all we don't know yet. To say that something follows a natural law is, for a theist, to say that God is the Creator of all, including natural laws.

Imagine the frustration that God must feel every time His followers are accused of saying "Godidit." Perhaps the following fable might give us a clue—though, as usual, I recommend not taking it *too* seriously.

A Fable About Science and Faith

The archangel Michael said to God, "Lord, some of the humans on earth are now saying that if something can be explained by science, then nobody needs to believe in You."

God was surprised. "But that simply makes no sense at all. What does one thing have to do with the other? Who do they think created their science in the first place? This is very frustrating. Let me speak to that Italian scientist."

Michael sent for Galileo, who appeared instantly. The Lord addressed him.

"Galileo, can you explain what your modern colleagues are up to? Don't they understand that when something has a scientific explanation, it only further adds to My glory and majesty? All you science people used to be My biggest fans."

Galileo bowed in respect and agreement. "Lord, I was speaking to Sir Isaac and a few others only yesterday. We are totally mystified by these new atheists and their worship of science instead of You."

"What do you suggest I do?"

Galileo thought for a long moment. "Lord, perhaps if you could help out some of the intelligent design people, you know, the ones who are trying to prove your existence scientifically . . ."

God shook His head emphatically. "No, no, no. Science cannot prove My existence—I created science. Also, their science is wrong, and we can't have that."

"But Lord, You must do something. People are starting to think that they must choose between believing in You and believing science." Galileo shook his head in concern. "Maybe You should ask Al."

"I knew you were going to say that. All right, send him in."

God sighed. Talking to Al was not His favorite thing to do.

Al sat down opposite God and, without any preamble, said, "Either we believe nothing is a miracle, or we believe everything is a miracle."

God rolled His eyes. "Al, are we going to go through this yet again? Look around you. Where do you think you are? Who do you think I am?"

Al was the only person in heaven who still claimed to be an agnostic, which was not pleasing to God. Al now suggested they play a game. "I brought my own dice," he said, but God glowered at him, since that whole dice thing was just a touch . . . dicey.

"What do you think about these atheists?" the Lord asked. "Anything we can do?"

"Nothing, Lord. The truth will always come out. These guys are starting to sound as rigid and unscientific as the young-earth people. Let them talk, let them publish, they will fade away in time. Right now they appear to be dangerous, but remember: everything is relative."

Now, even though God thought Al was an obnoxious show-off, He also knew that Al was usually right. So God decided to follow this advice and do nothing.

It was the right thing to do. Some years went by, and people began to see that science and faith were not only compatible but complementary and mutually supportive. Even some of the most fervent atheists eventually saw reason and began to worship the Creator of all of physics, chemistry, and biology.

Wisdom in Faith and Science

At the meetings and conferences I've attended in recent years, I have heard and met some of the true Christian heroes of our time like John Walton, Alister McGrath, and N. T. Wright. These giants of Christian theological scholarship are wise, humble, amazing people who have heard the call of Jesus to come and help Him lead His flock out of darkness and into the light of a new understanding of the Gospel and Scripture.

Werner Heisenberg's quote at the start of this chapter rings true for me as I contemplate my own journey (and that of many others). I think that there are three stages in the understanding of truth that a lot of people go through. As children or youngsters, they learn about the world from their parents' point of view. In many cases this includes a religious education, often fairly narrow and simplistic in nature, intended for young children.

As they grow and learn, many of these young people will rebel against what they see as an illogical, irrational, obscurantist way of thinking. They will feel liberated to enter a new world of light, truth, science, and reason. It is a very heady feeling, and most folks who experience that sense of liberation stay there.

But there is a third stage. Since I skipped the first one and was born into the second, I am familiar with going from there to this third stage, but many people have gone from stage one to stage two and then to stage three. In the third stage, which is reached after the glass of science has been drained, the wise person finds that reason is very good for a lot of things, but it doesn't quite do it all. There is something missing. It isn't the old guy with the beard he heard about as a child, but it is something that is not found in all the scientific reasoning he has come to embrace. It is spirituality, another dimension of human life that includes the essence of love and other things that are untouchable by science. It also includes the path to God.

We have a lot of work to do. Scripture can appear to be self-contradicting, as can science—let alone the two with each other. All this means is that we haven't gotten all of it right yet. Part of my own faith is the belief that God's truth is the only truth, and that we can grow in our understanding of that truth through scientific and theological work. At some point, it will become clear that all roads lead to this one truth.

I went to a scientific conference recently. I heard the talks as sermons. I saw the data charts on the slides as God's holy message. The speakers were like pastors, spreading the good news of God's creation. After each talk, I heard the applause as a loud amen. In the halls, my colleagues, the worshippers, wished each other peace and were thankful for the gifts of understanding and wonder the Lord had bestowed upon us. Old friends met and broke bread together. Praise be to the Lord whose every creation tells us of His glory, and thanks be to Him for revealing His secrets to us and allowing us to share all that knowledge and wisdom with the world in love.

CHAPTER 14

Alleluia

I KNEW THAT my journey was not finished when I came to worship Jesus Christ as my Lord and Redeemer. I wanted to be baptized and be part of a church. I wanted to take Holy Communion and learn more about Christianity. I was living in Milan, Italy, at the time, so I went to a Catholic church where I had heard there was an English service and the priest spoke English. (At that point, my church experiences had all been with Catholic churches.) I met with Father Giovanni and explained my situation. He was very kind and happy to meet with me on a regular basis. He gave me a copy of the then newly revised catechism of the Roman Catholic Church, which I enjoyed immensely. It was dense and long, but I found the language to be beautifully spiritual and soothing for the soul. I also enjoyed my talks with Father Giovanni. I had questions and he answered them.

One day he said to me, "If you have any questions left that are bothering you, that might stand in the way of your acceptance of the faith, let me know."

I thought about this for a moment. There *was* one. "I don't understand the Trinity. If God is one, how can He be three persons?"

He smiled and answered, "I have no answer for that. It is a mystery."

I smiled also. It was the perfect answer, and I knew I was ready.

In the end, I was not baptized in the Roman Catholic Church, and I did not become a Catholic. I tried twice, but it was not to be. Both in Milan and later in the United States, I found that while the Catholic Church had wonderful, caring priests, it also had a bureaucracy whose rules were sometimes more important than the bringing of a repentant sinner to Christ. I had led a complex and stormy life, and there were reasons (two different reasons for my two attempts, both related to previous marriages) that I was rejected. I prefer to say no more about this since I respect and admire the Catholic priests and laypeople I have met, and I hope that Pope Francis and future popes can continue to lead the Roman Catholic Church into a new day of Christian renewal, away from the stifling legacies of the past.

I gave up on ever being an "official" Christian for a few years. Then I moved to Maryland for a job, and I decided I would look into some Protestant churches in the area. I had never been in one, and I didn't know what to expect. One Sunday I walked into a Methodist church and sat down. The pastor gave a sermon that had me almost in tears—it was full of the truth of love as the guiding principle of Christ's teaching. I went back the next Sunday, and again I was moved and thrilled by the sermon. I spoke to Pastor Sue after the service, and she invited me to come see her during the week. I told her my story, and she smiled.

"Would you like to be baptized this Sunday?" she asked me.

I was stunned. "Sure," I said. "But don't I need to have some training, fill out some forms . . . ?"

She laughed. "All you need is the grace of the Holy Spirit, and you certainly have that."

So, in July 2012, I was finally baptized, and I joined the United

Methodist Church. I have attended services almost every Sunday since then, volunteered for a number of committees, organized events, and given classes about evolution and the science-and-faith dialogue. I am now the lay leader for my congregation as well as the lay delegate to the annual conference of the Baltimore-Washington Conference of the United Methodist Church.

I have learned that to grow toward maturity as a Christian, one must be a member of the body of Christ, the church. Sometimes I find myself sitting in a pew, praying my prayer of thanksgiving for all the blessings of my life, none of which I deserve, and I am overcome again by the same emotion I felt when I realized that Christ had called me to come to Him, to unwrap the gift of faith, and to join Him in eternal glory.

There is one final question that still needs to be answered.

Why Did I Write This Book?

I started with a joke, and I will end with one. It's from a cartoon in which a woman is telling her husband to get off his computer and go to bed. His answer is, "I can't . . . someone is wrong on the internet!" There is something inside me (the voice of the Holy Spirit, perhaps) that wants to correct all the mistakes I see people making in the media about science and faith. But I also know that I might be completely wrong about what I think is true and what I think is false. This book was not meant to be a series of lectures (although I realize that some chapters might come across that way—I am, after all, a professor). I am not interested in telling people what the truth is, because I don't ultimately know what the truth is.

Instead, I wrote this book as a story of how I came to be where I am today. I have told my story to individuals and to groups, and several people have told me I ought to write it down. A few even suggested a book. Eventually I felt called by Christ to do it.

Usually people put this section at the beginning of the book, not at the end. I assume you have read the rest of the book by now, and you have some thoughts about what you read. Perhaps your story is similar to mine, at least in some respects. Perhaps it's very different, but maybe you learned something about how the Holy Spirit can move in the strangest ways and in the least likely of people. Perhaps you know someone who is struggling with questions about science and faith for whom this book might provide some answers. Perhaps I have raised some questions that you have thought about, and you will look further for the answers.

The best philosophical understanding of modern science leads to faith in God.

I truly believe that the best philosophical understanding of modern science leads to faith in God and that a scientific understanding of nature can never be complete without the acknowledgment that the Creator of the universe is the Author of all. This is a radical idea in some circles and might not be ready for wide acceptance. I hope to delve into this idea further and, God willing, share what I find in the future.

I will close by thanking you for reading this far and for your patience with all my errors and failures in the book. I apologize for not being able to fully express the feelings in my heart or the joy of my soul. I know that I am a sinner, but I also know that I am redeemed by the love of Christ. I rejoice in the hope that some word or sentence in this book might have touched you in some way, healed your troubled mind, given you some degree of relief or even pleasure, or stimulated your mind to think about new ideas.

I would love to hear from you. Please visit my blog at thebookof works.com and tell me whatever you like. I am @sygarte on Twitter. Until then, may you go with the beauty of God's creation and the laws that govern it in your mind, the peace of Christ in your soul, and His sacrificial love in your heart. Alleluia and amen.

Acknowledgments

THERE ARE SO many people I would like to thank, people who lent me a hand during my journeys when I was stuck or just needed some love and support. I can't fit them all here, but the following are probably the most important. First are those who contributed to the existence of this book: my wife, Anikó Albert, who served as editor, chief critic, and general supporter when I needed it most, Mark Meredith, Elizabeth Hill, Denis Lamoureux, Perry Marshall, Darrel Falk, Dan Balow, Steve Laube, Joel Armstrong, Katherine Chappell, Steve Barclift, Noelle Pedersen, and of course, Alister McGrath.

Those who held out the Word of God for me on my faith journey: Gillian Stevens, Emanuela Taioli, Dave Abernathy, Father Giovanni (St. Carmine Church, Milan, Italy), Pastor Sue Brown (retired), Pastor Martha Meredith, and the congregation of the Rockville United Methodist Church.

There are so many who have helped guide me in my faith and science journey. Most I have not met, but those I have and whom I count as saints are Francis Collins, N. T. Wright, Simon Conway Morris, Agustín Fuentes, Jennifer Wiseman, Mike Beidler, Keith Furman, Paul Arveson, Randy Isaac, Vicki Best, Ted Davis, Jeff Schloss, Deb Haarsma, Kathryn Applegate, Brad Kramer, James Peterson, Tom Burnett, Jeff Greenberg, Se Kim, and Steven Freeland.

And those who at critical moments were there with support and encouragement: Kevin Arnold, Paul Wason, Michael Murray, Cherie Harder, Emily Ruppel Herrington, Ethan Ortega, Sheila Deeth, David Kent, Jon Garvey, and Ken Wolgemuth. This book project was made possible by a generous grant (#57657) from the John Templeton Foundation.

Finally, my family: Anikó, Giancarlo, Cora, Edna, Kevin, and Alex.

Appendix A: Discussion Questions

Chapter 1: The Importance of Questions
1. What questions have been important in your own life journey, and how have you found answers to them?
2. What questions do you still need answered about the big issues of life and the universe?
3. Which (if any) of the big questions posed in this chapter have you wrestled with, and what answers (if any) have you come up with?

Chapter 2: The Irrational World of Modern Physics
1. Before you read this chapter, how much did you know about the strange nature of modern physics?
2. What philosophical or theological implications come to mind in response to the modern discoveries about the physics of our universe?
3. If you could ask a physicist any question, what would it be? Why?

Chapter 3: Science Surprises
1. Which of the scientific concepts discussed in this chapter did you find most surprising, and why?
2. How does the fractal nature of just about everything change the way that you look at the natural world?
3. What experiences have you had with the chaotic nature of complex systems such as the weather, market forces, and political and social trends?

Chapter 4: Wonderful Life

1. If you could make a new discovery about the mysterious details of biology, what would you research? (For more technical material on biology, see appendix C.)
2. Are you convinced that the complexity of the biochemical processes of life indicate the presence of a divine designer? If so, why? If not, why not?
3. Do you think, based on what you read in this chapter, that life might arise without divine intervention wherever the conditions for it exist? If not, why not?

Chapter 5: There Is Grandeur—Darwin's Evolution

1. After reading this chapter, have your ideas and feelings about the subject of evolution changed? How so?
2. What new information about evolution did you learn from this chapter?
3. Do you agree that evolution is a strong pointer to God's creative majesty? Discuss this idea from a scriptural context.

Chapter 6: People

1. Which points about the nature of humanity made in this chapter do you agree with, and which do you disagree with?
2. What is your view of the meaning of *imago Dei*? How do the implications of this chapter challenge or align with your view of God's image in humanity?
3. What do you wish we knew more about concerning how humans came to be the way that we are?

Chapter 7: Origins

1. What were your previous ideas about origins (of the universe, life, and humanity) before reading this chapter? Have any of them changed? How?

2. Which parts of this chapter do you disagree with, and why?

3. What scientific aspects of this chapter do you wish there were time to explore more thoroughly?

Chapter 8: The Limits of Science

1. What are some examples of scientism that strike you as particularly fallacious?

2. What do you see as the limits of scientific knowledge, and what other forms of knowing (epistemology) are or are not necessary?

3. What kinds of "stop signs" have you run into in your life?

Chapter 9: The Call of Faith

1. Have you experienced any dreams, visions, or inspirational thoughts that influenced how you felt about God, faith, or any part of your personal life? If comfortable doing so, consider sharing them and what impact they had on you with another person or the group.

2. When did you know that you were a follower of Christ, or realize that your doubts had led you to disbelief?

3. Do you believe in the intervention of the Holy Spirit in your daily life? What evidence have you experienced?

Chapter 10: But What About . . . ?

1. Which parts of this chapter (if any) resonate with your own experiences? What discussions or arguments have you had with others about these issues?

2. Which parts of this chapter (if any) are you uncomfortable with or disagree with? Why?

3. When and if someone starts arguing with you about your faith, what arguments do they use the most? How do you answer them?

Chapter 11: Love and Freedom, Chance and Will

1. What is your own answer to the problem of evil?
2. What are your reactions to the discussions on free will and chance? Discuss these issues and their relationship to Christian faith.
3. What do you think is the importance of love in relation to everything else, especially from a scriptural viewpoint?

Chapter 12: Evolution and Christianity

1. What impact does the extended evolutionary synthesis (EES) have on your thoughts about evolution?
2. Have you previously heard about evolutionary creationism? What are your reactions about this viewpoint of creation in a Christian context?
3. What surprised you about what evolution does *not* mean?

Chapter 13: Science and Faith Together

1. What were your thoughts about the conflict between science and religion before reading this book? Have they changed now?
2. What do you want to learn more about concerning the interface between science and faith? (Check out resources like Francis Collins's *The Language of God* and websites like BioLogos and the American Scientific Affiliation listed in appendix B.)
3. Which (if any) of the conclusions of this chapter, and the book in general, would you consider discussing in a church setting or with other Christians?

Chapter 14: Alleluia

1. What overall impact has this book made on your thoughts and feelings about Christianity, science, life, and love?
2. What prayer would you say to further the work of those de-

voted to discovering and promoting the idea that science is not an enemy but a servant of God?

3. What can you do to support those struggling to convince the world that Christianity is not the enemy of science but that they must go together to allow for the fullest understanding of the beauty of our natural world?

Appendix B: Further Reading

Alexander, Denis. *Is There Purpose in Biology? The Cost of Existence and the God of Love*. Oxford: Lion Hudson, 2018.

Applegate, Kathryn, and J. B. Stump, eds. *How I Changed My Mind About Evolution: Evangelicals Reflect on Faith and Science*. Downers Grove, IL: IVP Academic, 2016.

Barrigar, Christian J. *Freedom All the Way Up: God and the Meaning of Life in a Scientific Age*. Victoria, BC: Friesen, 2017.

Collins, Francis S. *The Language of God: A Scientist Presents Evidence for Belief*. New York: Free Press, 2006.

Darwin, Charles. *Journal of Researches*. New York: American Dome Library, 1902.

———. *On the Origin of Species by Means of Natural Selection, or the Preservation of Favoured Races in the Struggle for Life*. New York: Modern Library, 1993. Originally published in 1859.

Davidson, Gregg. *Friend of Science, Friend of Faith: Listening to God in His Works and Word*. Grand Rapids: Kregel Academic, 2019.

Dawkins, Richard. *A Devil's Chaplain: Reflections on Hope, Lies, Science, and Love*. Boston: Mariner, 2004.

Dawkins, Richard, and Yan Wong. *The Ancestor's Tale: A Pilgrimage to the Dawn of Evolution*. New York: Mariner, 2016.

Diamond, Jared. *The Third Chimpanzee: The Evolution and Future of the Human Animal*. New York: HarperCollins, 1992.

Falk, Darrel R. *Coming to Peace with Science: Bridging the Worlds Between Faith and Biology*. Downers Grove, IL: InterVarsity, 2004.

Garvey, Jon. *God's Good Earth: The Case for an Unfallen Creation.* Eugene, OR: Cascade Books, 2019.

Giberson, Karl W. *Saving Darwin: How to Be a Christian and Believe in Evolution.* San Francisco: HarperOne, 2008.

Giberson, Karl W., and Francis S. Collins. *The Language of Science and Faith: Straight Answers to Genuine Questions.* Downers Grove, IL: InterVarsity, 2011.

Gould, Paul M., and Daniel Ray, eds. *The Story of the Cosmos: How the Heavens Declare the Glory of God.* Eugene, OR: Harvest House, 2019.

Haarsma, Deborah B., and Loren D. Haarsma. *Origins: Christian Perspectives on Creation, Evolution, and Intelligent Design.* 2nd ed. Grand Rapids: Faith Alive Christian Resources, 2011.

Hill, Carol, Gregg Davidson, Tim Helble, and Wayne Ranney, eds. *The Grand Canyon, Monument to an Ancient Earth: Can Noah's Flood Explain the Grand Canyon?* Grand Rapids: Kregel, 2016.

Hutchinson, Ian. *Monopolizing Knowledge: A Scientist Refutes Religion-Denying, Reason-Destroying Scientism.* Belmont, MA: Fias, 2011.

Kumar, Manjit. *Quantum: Einstein, Bohr, and the Great Debate About the Nature of Reality.* New York: W. W. Norton, 2008.

Lamoureux, Denis O. *Evolution: Scripture and Nature Say Yes!* Grand Rapids: Zondervan, 2016.

———. *I Love Jesus and I Accept Evolution.* Eugene, OR: Wipf and Stock, 2009.

Lewis, C. S. *Mere Christianity.* New York: HarperCollins, 1952.

———. *Miracles: How God Intervenes in Nature and Human Affairs.* New York: MacMillan, 1978. Originally published in 1947.

Marshall, Perry. *Evolution 2.0: Breaking the Deadlock Between Darwin and Design.* Dallas: BenBella, 2015.

McGrath, Alister. *Dawkins' God: Genes, Memes, and the Meaning of Life*. Malden, MA: Blackwell, 2007.

———. *Science and Religion: A New Introduction*. 2nd ed. Chichester: Wiley-Blackwell, 2009.

McGrath, Alister, and Joanna Collicutt McGrath. *The Dawkins Delusion? Atheist Fundamentalism and the Denial of the Divine*. Downers Grove, IL: InterVarsity, 2007.

Miller, Keith B., ed. *Perspectives on an Evolving Creation*. Grand Rapids: Eerdmans, 2003.

Morris, Simon Conway. *Life's Solution: Inevitable Humans in a Lonely Universe*. New York: Cambridge University Press, 2003.

Murphy, George L. *The Cosmos in the Light of the Cross*. Harrisburg, PA: Trinity Press International, 2003.

Noble, Denis. *Dance to the Tune of Life: Biological Relativity*. Cambridge: Cambridge University Press, 2017.

Oord, Thomas J. *The Uncontrolling Love of God: An Open and Relational Account of Providence*. Downers Grove, IL: IVP Academic, 2015.

Rees, Martin. *Just Six Numbers: The Deep Forces That Shape the Universe*. New York: Basic Books, 2000.

Ross, Hugh. *The Creator and the Cosmos: How the Latest Scientific Discoveries Reveal God*. 4th ed. Covina, CA: Reasons to Believe, 2018.

Tegmark, Max. *Our Mathematical Universe: My Quest for the Ultimate Nature of Reality*. New York: Vintage Books, 2015.

Venema, Dennis R., and Scot McKnight. *Adam and the Genome: Reading Scripture After Genetic Science*. Grand Rapids: Brazos, 2017.

Wagner, Andreas. *Arrival of the Fittest: How Nature Innovates*. New York: Current, 2015.

Walsh, Andy. *Faith Across the Multiverse: Parables from Modern Science*. Peabody, MA: Hendrickson, 2018.

Walton, John H. *The Lost World of Adam and Eve: Genesis 2–3 and the Human Origins Debate*. Downers Grove, IL: IVP Academic, 2015.

————. *The Lost World of Genesis One: Ancient Cosmology and the Origins Debate*. Downers Grove, IL: IVP Academic, 2009.

Whitcomb, John C., and Henry M. Morris. *The Genesis Flood: The Biblical Record and Its Scientific Implications*. 50th anniversary ed. Phillipsburg, NJ: P&R, 2011.

Wood, Todd Charles, and Darrel R. Falk. *The Fool and the Heretic: How Two Scientists Moved Beyond Labels to a Christian Dialogue About Creation and Evolution*. Grand Rapids: Zondervan, 2019.

Wright, N. T. *Surprised by Scripture: Engaging Contemporary Issues*. San Francisco: HarperOne, 2014.

Appendix C: The Details of Life

THIS APPENDIX PROVIDES more details about the information presented in chapters 4–6 for those readers with an interest in biology and evolution. They may also consult the books listed in appendix B or find many other good resources online. The material presented here is not at all comprehensive. Its purpose is to fill in some details in the more general overviews presented in the main body of the book.

More Details on Molecular Biology

Transcription: How Information Is Copied from DNA into RNA

The DNA in a cell is the molecule that stores the coded information (see genetic code later) needed to produce all the cellular proteins. The DNA is arranged in a helical structure, in which two strands of sugars and phosphates attached to the coding bases wind around each other. This structure, called a "double helix" by its discoverers, James Watson and Francis Crick, allows the bases on the two strands to interact.

Coded information in the form of base sequences is copied from the DNA (*deoxyribonucleic acid*) base sequence into a related molecule called RNA (*ribonucleic acid*), which then leaves the nucleus (where the DNA remains like a bound book) and is processed in tiny protein-making machines called ribosomes. An analogy would be making a photocopy of one page of a large book of instructions on how to build a house so that the workers at the building site can consult the instructions as they work. The copying of the instructions from DNA to RNA is a chemical process that involves many enzymes. The enzymes build a chain of RNA that is a perfect sequence match to one of the two DNA strands in the double helix. This RNA is called messenger RNA (mRNA), since it literally serves as a message from the central information repository to the protein factory.

Amino Acids and Proteins

Proteins, like DNA, are long polymers. But they are very different from DNA in most other aspects of their chemistry. First, they are made of subunits of amino acids, not bases. They have no rigid structure like the sugars and phosphates of DNA, but once formed, they fold and compress and form all kinds of structures. And there are not four kinds of amino acids but twenty.

The beauty of amino acids lies in their diverse chemical potentials for reactions. All amino acids share a common chemical structure but also contain many different chemical groups, ranging from a simple single hydrogen atom to complex ring structures. The result of all this variety is an unlimited degree of possibility for chemical reactivities by the proteins. This is why proteins are the best, most versatile, and most adaptive chemical catalysts ever seen.

Translation or Protein Synthesis According to Coded Information

The individual amino acids of proteins and the bases of DNA or RNA do not interact or recognize each other chemically. If you mixed a batch of all twenty amino acids with DNA, RNA, or the bases that they are made of, nothing would happen, just like my very first chemistry experiment. So we are left with a difficult question. How in the world can a sequence of four DNA bases produce a long protein composed of twenty amino acids in just the right order when no chemical interaction between the two kinds of chemicals is possible?

The answer is a remarkable process that resembles a complex assembly system on a microscopic level. Every cell on earth, every plant, animal, and bacterium, works the same way to convert genetic information into phenotype. I don't know of any human-designed process that is so elaborate, so elegant, and so beautiful.

No less glorious (and no less complex) is the process by which the messenger RNA, the ribosome, and the transfer RNAs all work together to make the new protein with just the right amino acid sequence as mandated by the instructions in the DNA sequence.

All of the steps in the process are highly susceptible to error. Since errors are not tolerable here (and in fact the error rate in translation is extremely low), there exists an additional, complex system of error avoidance and correction that uses a host of special enzymes.

Many different chemical structures are involved in the process. The key players are three types of RNA molecules, an amazing enzyme (a protein), and the twenty amino acids. The cellular factories for making proteins are called ribosomes. They are large structures made of RNA. Ribosomes also act like an enzyme (a ribozyme), meaning that they catalyze a crucial reaction in the process. A close look at a ribosome reveals that it is composed of two units that fit together, with a groove in between them.

The messenger RNA molecule, carrying the precise sequence of nucleotides copied from the gene, leaves the nucleus and travels through the cytoplasm to the ribosome, where it gets wedged into the groove between the two units.

There are two types of crucial molecules that function as the adapters that actually do the work of translating one type of chemical message in the mRNA into the other chemical message of the protein sequence. One is called transfer RNA (tRNA) and the other is called aminoacyl tRNA synthetase (aaRS). The tRNA is made of

RNA, and the amino acid synthase is a protein enzyme. But there is not only one of each of these key molecules, there are twenty different kinds—one for each amino acid.

The most striking thing about the process is the tRNA. Unlike the messenger RNA, which is a long chain containing a coded message in its nucleotide sequence, the tRNA is a folded structure with a shape that is different in each of the twenty varieties. The valine tRNA looks nothing like the glycine tRNA. And each tRNA has another important feature. It has a three-nucleotide region (called the anticodon) that is exactly complementary to the codon for its amino acid. So if the codon for valine is ACG, the anticodon on the valine tRNA will read TGC. What this means is that the tRNA for valine can easily bind to the part of the mRNA that is coding for valine.

Each tRNA also has a binding site for an amino acid. But there is no way for any tRNA to recognize and bind to the amino acid that matches its anticodon, and in fact many different amino acids could be chemically bound to any tRNA.

This is where the aaRS (or AA SYN) enzymes come in. Again, there is one for each tRNA. These amazing enzymes have two separate binding sites, one for a specific tRNA (based on its shape) and one for the correct amino acid (the one that is coded for according to the anticodon on the other end of the tRNA). This is shown in figure 1.

So a single glycine aaRS will bind to the amino acid glycine in one place and to the tRNA for glycine in another place. As you can see in figure 2, once the correct amino acid and its tRNA are bound to their specific sites on the aaRS, the enzyme changes its shape and brings the two molecules together. The enzyme then catalyzes a chemical reaction that binds the amino acid directly to the tRNA. There is now a bond forming a "conjugate" between an amino acid and the anticodon on the tRNA that is meant for it. The two different chemical worlds of amino acids (protein chemistry) and nucleotides (DNA/RNA chemistry) have finally been linked together.

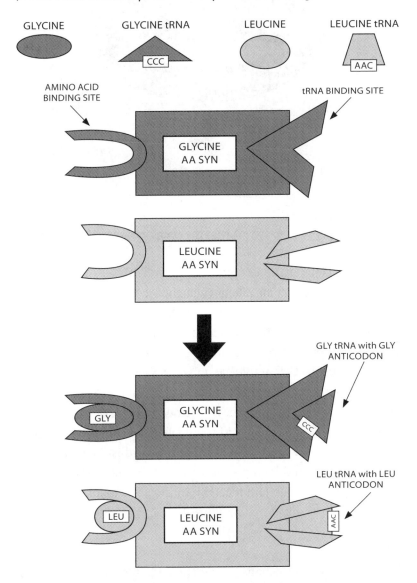

Figure 1. The aaRS enzyme binds an amino acid and its tRNA

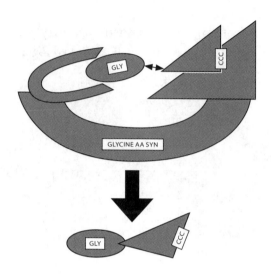

Figure 2. The enzyme joins the amino acid to its tRNA

The next steps are no less glorious. As you can see in figure 3, the tRNA–amino acid conjugate goes to the ribosome, where the linear tape of the mRNA is waiting. The tRNAs attach to the mRNA by codon-anticodon binding one at a time. When two tRNAs are present at the same time, the amino acids riding on top of them are stuck together by the catalytic action of the ribosome. At that point, the mRNA moves along the ribosome just one step, and the first tRNA is removed. The second tRNA now occupies the first position and another tRNA–amino acid conjugate takes the second position opposite the third codon. The third amino acid is then attached to the second one, and on it goes as one after another tRNAs bind to their codons and then join together amino acids to form a growing protein chain as illustrated in figure 4.

The Genetic Code

The universal and unchanging genetic code specifies which three-base sequence (called a codon) signifies the amino acid in the protein coded for by a gene. The code is presented in the following table (figure 5). An illustration of how the code works, and what happens when there is a mutation in the DNA sequence, is presented after the code table on the following page. The code table presents the codons (where T in DNA is replaced by U in RNA), followed by the three-letter symbols for the coded amino acid. Thus, for example, the codons UUC and UUU both code for the amino acid

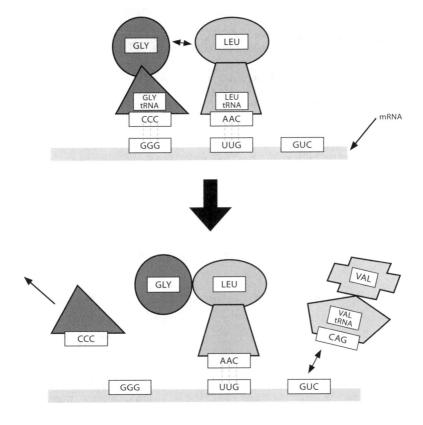

**Figure 3. A rough schematic of what happens at the
ribosome as proteins are made**

Protein Sequence	GLY LEU VAL SER LEU TRP ...
tRNA Anticodon	CCC AAC CAG AGU AAC ACC ...
mRNA Codon	GGG UUG GUC UCA UUG UGG ...
DNA Sequence	CCCAACCAGAGTAACACC ...

**Figure 4. A portion of a new protein with the amino acid sequence
following the DNA sequence; also showing the codons and anticodons
for each amino acid (T in DNA = U in RNA)**

phenylalanine (Phe). Notice that most amino acids are coded for
by more than one codon, but each codon only codes for one amino
acid. Also, UAA, UAG, and UGA are stop codons, which signal the
translation machinery to terminate and signify the end of a protein.

More Details on Evolution

Genetic Evidence for Evolution—The GULO Pseudogene
In mammals, there are a number of different gene sequences for the
GULO gene, which makes vitamin C. In the rat, the gene makes
a protein, and rats can make vitamin C. In primates, including
chimps and humans, there was a deletion of one base, the C at position 8 (see the table on page 244). The deletion caused a frameshift
mutation, so that the entire sequence after the gap shifts to the left.
The original codon GCG, which normally codes for alanine, is now
GGA (glycine). And the following codon, which was ATG in the rat,
coding for threonine, is now TGA, one of the three stop codons, and

Second Letter					
	U	C	A	G	

First Letter		Second Letter U	Second Letter C	Second Letter A	Second Letter G	Third Letter
	U	UUU ⎤ Phe UUC ⎦ UUA ⎤ Leu UUG ⎦	UCU ⎤ UCC UCA ⎦ Ser UCG	UAU ⎤ Tyr UAC ⎦ UAA ⎤ STOP UAG ⎦	UGU ⎤ Cys UGC ⎦ UGA — STOP UGG — Trp	U C A G
	C	CUU ⎤ CUC CUA ⎦ Leu CUG	CCU ⎤ CCC CCA ⎦ Pro CCG	CAU ⎤ His CAC ⎦ CAA ⎤ Gln CAG ⎦	CGU ⎤ CGC CGA ⎦ Arg CGG	U C A G
	A	AUU ⎤ AUC ⎦ Ile AUA ⎦ AUG — Met or Start	ACU ⎤ ACC ACA ⎦ Thr ACG	AAU ⎤ Asn AAC ⎦ AAA ⎤ Lys AAG ⎦	AGU ⎤ Ser AGC ⎦ AGA ⎤ Arg AGG ⎦	U C A G
	G	GUU ⎤ GUC GUA ⎦ Val GUG	GCU ⎤ GCC GCA ⎦ Ala GCG	GAU ⎤ Asp GAC ⎦ GAA ⎤ Glu GAG ⎦	GGU ⎤ GGC GGA ⎦ Gly GGG	U C A G

Sarah Greenwood (https://creativecommons.org/licenses/by-sa/4.0)

Figure 5. The genetic code

therefore the protein production ends too early and the enzyme doesn't work. So chimps (and all primates) have a nonworking pseudogene here and cannot synthesize vitamin C. In humans the pseudogene has also undergone additional mutations, such as the one shown here, where GAG (glutamic acid) has been mutated twice to GGA (glycine). Pseudogenes have no active function in the life of an organism and are therefore no longer under selection. This means that organisms with pseudogene mutations will not suffer any ill consequences, and therefore such mutations will be found at a higher frequency in the surviving population than mutations in normal, active genes. The table shows that an early primate underwent this specific deletion mutation, and it was passed down to all modern primates, including humans.

	Sequence Homology	Final Coding Sequence	Amino Acid Coded For
RAT	...CCC GAG GCG ATG ACA ...	...CCC GAG GCG ATG ...	...PRO GLU ALA THR ...
CHIMP	...CCT GAG G G ATG ACA ...	...CCT GAG GGA TGA ...	...PRO GLU GLY STOP ...
HUMAN	...CCT GGA G G ATG ACA ...	...CCT GGA GGA TGA ...	...PRO GLY GLY STOP ...

Details on the Extended Evolutionary Synthesis (EES)

Over the past decades, microbiologist James Shapiro has applied many findings on how cells can accomplish major genomic alterations to develop a model he calls natural genetic engineering. Shapiro's view is that the cell can control the genome as much as the genome controls the cell. When applied to evolution, these sources of genetic variation are rapid and dramatic, and involve grand molecular events, such as transposition of DNA sections leading to massive reengineering of proteins.

Various DNA sequence alterations are now known to play powerful roles in mutation. Gene duplication is a kind of mutation that can happen during cell division when a stretch of DNA is copied more than once. The result of this error is two or more copies of the same gene. This is important for evolution because one of the two copies has the "freedom" to mutate since its twin gene will continue to carry on the required function. In most cases the gene copy that freely mutates will eventually become a useless pseudogene, but sometime the greatly mutated extra copy will take on a new and useful function.

There is strong evidence that a whole genome duplication (WGD) event occurred at about the time of the origin of the vertebrates. The resulting large set of extra, highly mutated genes eventually became the source for new genes with new functions and entirely new ways of constructing the body plans and functions of living creatures. There is evidence that WGD events have occurred in flowering plants, at the origin of modern fish, and at other evolutionary transition points.

Another example of genetic mutation is the recent discovery of small DNA sections that can "jump" from one part of the genome to another. Called *transposons*, they are observed in the genomes of many species and have been shown to play a role in gene duplication throughout evolutionary history.

In 1988, a paper by molecular biologist John Cairns and his colleagues showed that bacteria could produce beneficial mutations targeted to specific genes in order to relieve severe stress. Cairns's paper took a major step away from the "purely random" concept for mutation. These beneficial mutations (now called stress-directed mutations) are produced at rates up to five times higher than neutral mutations. Numerous researchers have confirmed this phenomenon and have found a number of molecular mechanisms to account for it.

From the evidence of all these new ways to produce biological variation, it is now indisputable that evolution is far more complex, directed, and beautiful than the classical neo-Darwinian modern synthesis model suggests.

Appendix D: Discovering Darwin's Letter

In 1991, on a professional trip to London, I had some free time and went to the British Library. One of my hobbies is the collection of old science books, and I wondered what I might find at what is probably the world's most famous library. As I walked through the exhibition rooms, I saw a lot of manuscripts on display, but nothing on science. I asked a guard for directions to the scientific manuscripts, meaning some room where they might be on display. He seemed puzzled, but he was polite and helpful.

"What do you mean, sir?"

"Like Newton," I said, feeling hopelessly American in a civilized country. "Isaac Newton," I added for clarity.

"Ah," he said. "Are you a scholar, sir?"

Tough question. I decided to throw modesty to the wind. "Yes, I'm a professor in New York."

He smiled and asked me to follow him, which seemed strange. I thought, *Jeez, all I want to know is where to find the science section.*

We passed through a door and entered a guarded corridor. The second guard, even friendlier than the first, was told that the American scholar was interested in seeing some manuscripts of Isaac Newton's. I spoke to someone who gave me a one-day pass to view any manuscript in the catalog. Since I had originally mentioned Isaac Newton, I was brought into the manuscript reading room and given a bound book containing a large variety of letters and other documents from the sixteenth century. Several pages were original manuscripts of Isaac Newton's (in Latin) on ancient solar and lunar calendars, including a table of calculations. This was breathtaking. I actually had the original Isaac Newton manuscript in my hand! When I was able to come to my senses, I realized what an incredible opportunity I had.

I looked up Darwin in the catalog and found that there was a file of over three hundred pages of correspondence between Darwin and Alfred Russel Wallace. I had to fight against some strong emotion and a growing conviction that this was too good to be true. It wasn't. I was given the collection, and I began to go through it with all the reverence a priest would feel looking at an original manuscript written by the apostle Paul.

Darwin's letters were all handwritten on small quartered sheets (both sides of the paper) and many were not dated. Wallace's letters were typed blue carbon copies. This told me that the collection had come from Wallace.

I leafed through these letters with a great deal of pleasure. Some of Darwin's notes were barely legible, which didn't surprise me, since I knew that during his fits of illness, writing became difficult for him. I was skimming through some of the later letters when one caught my attention. It was written on a folded notepaper with a black border. I surmised that Darwin, looking for something to write on, had used a handy funeral announcement or sympathy stationary.

The letter is short, and it contains part of an ongoing discussion with Wallace about heredity. At that time no one knew anything about heredity of genes except Mendel, and Mendel's work had been all but lost. Everything I had ever read about Darwin maintained that he, like everyone else at the time, believed that the inheritance of characteristics was like mixing paint colors—that the characteristics of both parents were blended together in the children. Yet in this letter (from 1866), Darwin writes (the following is the complete handwritten text of the letter):

Down Bromley SE
Tuesday

My dear Wallace
   After I had dispatched my last note, the simple explanation which you give had occurred to me, & seems
satisfactory.
   I do not think you understand what I mean by the non-
blending of certain varieties. It does not refer to fertil-
ity; an instance will explain; I crossed the Painted Lady
& Purple sweet-peas, which are very differently coloured
vars, & got, even out of the same pod, both varieties perfect but none intermediate. Something of this kind I sh^d
think must occur at first with your butterflies & the three
forms of Lythrum; tho' these cases are in appearance so
wonderful, I do not know that they are really more so
than every female in this world producing distinct male &
female offspring. I am heartily glad that you mean to go on
preparing your journal. Believe me—yours very sincerely
Ch. Darwin

In other words, Darwin is telling Wallace that he crossed two different color pea plants and got only one or the other color, not any
mixed or in-between varieties. He is describing quantum inheritance: genes. (And he was in fact using the same methodology as
Mendel.) I read the letter over and over again. Darwin knew about
genes! This was the first indication I had seen (or that anyone else
had seen, for that matter) that Darwin had some inkling about the
real mechanism of genetic inheritance, and I thought that it was a
pretty important finding.
   I sent a copy of the letter to Richard Dawkins (whom I admired
as a leading proponent of evolution), and he later discussed this

letter (and kindly gave me credit for its discovery) in an essay in *A Devil's Chaplain.*[1]

The best part of the story is my imagining Charles Darwin sitting in heaven and, like all scientists, paying close attention to the literature of the past century. I am sure he has followed the development of the field of genetics with great satisfaction, since the research confirms and provides a firm framework for his theory of evolution by natural selection. But I can also imagine him being a bit frustrated by the fact that he was so close to seeing the whole truth himself—and the evidence of how close he came had been locked away in a single letter in the British Library for over a hundred years. As the person who had the honor and privilege of bringing this letter to light, I feel that Darwin's spirit is smiling down on me. Nothing could top that.

Notes

Chapter 1: The Importance of Questions
1. Albert Michelson, "The Department of Physics," in *Annual Register: July, 1895–July, 1896* (Chicago: University of Chicago Press, 1896), 159.

Chapter 2: The Irrational World of Modern Physics
1. Manjit Kumar, *Quantum: Einstein, Bohr, and the Great Debate About the Nature of Reality* (New York: W. W. Norton, 2011), 248.
2. Roger Penrose, foreword to *Quo Vadis Quantum Mechanics?*, ed. Avshalom C. Elitzur, Shahar Dolev, and Nancy Kolenda, Frontier Collection (Berlin: Springer, 2005), vii–viii.
3. Martin Rees, "The Anthropic Universe," *New Scientist*, August 6, 1987, 46.
4. Max Born, ed., *The Born-Einstein Letters: The Correspondence Between Albert Einstein and Max and Hedwig Born 1916–1955* (New York: Walker & Company, 1971), 158.
5. Brian Clegg, *The God Effect: Quantum Entanglement, Science's Strangest Phenomenon* (New York: St. Martin's Press, 2006).
6. Niels Bohr, quoted in Werner Heisenberg, *Physics and Beyond: Encounters and Conversations*, trans. Arnold J. Pomerans (London: George Allen & Unwin, 1971), 88.
7. David Bohm, *Wholeness and the Implicate Order* (Abington, UK: Routledge, 2002), 173. Emphasis in original.

Chapter 3: Science Surprises
1. Seymour Garte, "Fractal Properties of the Human Genome,"

Journal of Theoretical Biology 230, no. 2 (September 2004): 251–60, https://doi.org/10.1016/j.jtbi.2004.05.015.

2. Stephen Hawking and Leonard Mlodinow, *The Grand Design* (New York: Bantam, 2010), 162.

3. Sabine Hossenfelder, "The Uncertain Future of Particle Physics," *New York Times*, January 23, 2019, https://www.nytimes.com/2019/01/23/opinion/particle-physics-large-hadron-collider.html.

Chapter 5: There Is Grandeur—Darwin's Evolution

1. Sy Garte, "Teleology and the Origin of Evolution," *Perspectives on Science and Christian Faith* 69, no. 1 (March 2017): 42–50, https://www.asa3.org/ASA/PSCF/2017/PSCF3-17Garte.pdf.

2. Jason Philip Downs, Edward B. Daeschler, Farish A. Jenkins Jr., and Neil H. Shubin, "The Cranial Endoskeleton of *Tiktaalik roseae*," *Nature* 455 (October 2008): 925–29, https://doi.org/10.1038/nature07189.

3. Daniel C. Dennett, "Evolution, Teleology, Intentionality," *Behavioral and Brain Sciences* 16, no. 2 (June 1993): 389–91, https://doi.org/10.1017/S0140525X00030697.

4. Garte, "Teleology and the Origin of Evolution," 48–49. Emphasis in original.

5. Perry Marshall, "Are Cells Intelligent?," *Evolution 2.0* (blog), accessed September 3, 2019, https://evo2.org/cells-intelligent/.

Chapter 6: People

1. Jerry Coyne, "The Smithsonian Does Theology," *Why Evolution Is True* (blog), February 26, 2016, https://whyevolutionis
true.wordpress.com/2016/02/26/the-smithsonian-does-theology
-sets-us-committee-to-promote-accommodationism-and-show
-no-disparity-between-religious-and-scientific-views-of-human
-origins. Emphasis in original.

2. Sy Garte, "Evolution and Imago Dei," *God & Nature* 1, no. 3

(Fall 2012), http://godandnature.asa3.org/essay-evolution-and
-imago-dei.html.

3. Pascal Gagneux et al., "Mitochondrial Sequences Show Diverse
Evolutionary Histories of African Hominoids," *Proceedings of
the National Academy of Sciences* 96, no. 9 (April 1999): 5077–
82, https://doi.org/10.1073/pnas.96.9.5077.

4. Stanley H. Ambrose, "Did the Super-Eruption of Toba Cause a
Human Population Bottleneck? Reply to Gathorne-Hardy and
Harcourt-Smith," *Journal of Human Evolution* 45, no. 3 (2003):
231–37, https://doi.org/10.1016/j.jhevol.2003.08.001.

5. Jared Diamond, *The Third Chimpanzee: The Evolution and Future of the Human Animal* (New York: HarperCollins, 1992), 82.

Chapter 7: Origins

1. Yuri I. Wolf and Eugene V. Koonin, "On the Origin of the
Translation System and the Genetic Code in the RNA World
by Means of Natural Selection, Exaptation, and Subfunctional-
ization," *Biology Direct* 2, no. 14 (May 2007), 4, https://biology
direct.biomedcentral.com/track/pdf/10.1186/1745-6150-2-14.

2. See George F. R. Ellis, "Top-Down Causation and Emergence:
Some Comments on Mechanisms," *Interface Focus* 2, no. 1 (February 2012): 126–40, https://doi.org/10.1098/rsfs.2011.0062.

3. *The Genius of Charles Darwin*, episode 2, "The Fifth Ape,"
directed by Russell Barnes, written by Richard Dawkins, aired
August 11, 2008, on Channel 4.

4. Daniel C. Dennett, *Consciousness Explained* (Boston: Back
Bay Books, 1991).

Chapter 8: The Limits of Science

1. S. C. Kleene, "On the Interpretation of Intuitionistic Number
Theory," *Journal of Symbolic Logic* 10, no. 4 (December 1945):
109–24, https://doi.org/10.2307/2269016.

2. Johannes Koelman, "Limits to Science: God, Godel, Gravity,"

Science 2.0, November 12, 2010, https://www.science20.com /hammock_physicist/limits_science_god_godel_gravity.

3. D. F. Eggers Jr., N. W. Gregory, G. D. Halsey Jr., B. S. Rabinovitch, *Physical Chemistry* (Hoboken, NJ: John Wiley & Sons, 1964), 23.

4. Kenneth Denbigh, *The Principles of Chemical Equilibrium: With Applications in Chemistry and Chemical Engineering*, 4th ed. (Cambridge: Cambridge University Press, 1981), 111.

5. Venkat Srinivasan, "Are the Constants of Physics Constant?" *Scientific American* (blog), March 7, 2016, https://blogs.scientific american.com/guest-blog/are-the-constants-of-physics-constant/.

Chapter 10: But What About . . . ?

1. Albert Mohler, "Creation Vs. Evolution—The New Shape of the Debate," AlbertMohler.com, February 1, 2011, https://albertmohler .com/2011/02/01/creation-vs-evolution-the-new-shape-of-the-debate.

2. Pope Benedict XVI, *"In the Beginning . . .": A Catholic Understanding of the Story of Creation and the Fall* (Grand Rapids: Eerdmans, 1995), 4–5, 50. Emphasis in original.

3. "Religious Landscape Study: Views About Human Evolution," Pew Research Center, 2014, http://www.pewforum.org /religious-landscape-study/views-about-human-evolution/.

4. "Religious Landscape Study," Pew Research Center.

5. C. S. Lewis, "Is Theology Poetry?," *The Weight of Glory*, rev. ed. (San Francisco: HarperOne, 2001), 135.

Chapter 12: Evolution and Christianity

1. Richard Dawkins, *The Blind Watchmaker: Why the Evidence of Evolution Reveals a Universe Without Design* (New York: W. W. Norton, 2015), 10.

2. "Religious Landscape Study: Views About Human Evolution," Pew Research Center, 2014, http://www.pewforum.org /religious-landscape-study/views-about-human-evolution/.

3. Charles Darwin, *On the Origin of Species by Means of Natural*

Selection, or the Preservation of Favoured Races in the Struggle for Life (1859; repr., New York: Modern Library, 1993), 172.

4. Denis Alexander, "Made in the Image of God: Human Values and Genomics," *HuffPost*, January 10, 2013, https://www.huffingtonpost.com/dr-denis-alexander/made-in-the-image-of-god-human-value-and-human-genomics_b_2401494.html.

5. Sy Garte, "New Ideas in Evolutionary Biology: From NDMS to EES," *Perspectives on Science and Christian Faith* 68, no. 1 (March 2016): 3–11, https://www.asa3.org/ASA/PSCF/2016/PSCF3-16Garte.pdf.

6. Stephen Jay Gould, *Wonderful Life: The Burgess Shale and the Nature of History* (New York: W. W. Norton, 2007), 14.

7. "What We Believe," BioLogos, accessed August 8, 2019, https://biologos.org/about-us/what-we-believe/. Used by permission.

8. Eugenie C. Scott, "Antievolution and Creationism in the United States," *Annual Review of Anthropology* 26 (1997): 263–89.

9. Sy Garte, "Teleology and the Origin of Evolution," *Perspectives on Science and Christian Faith* 69, no. 1 (March 2017): 42–50, https://www.asa3.org/ASA/PSCF/2017/PSCF3-17Garte.pdf. Emphasis in original.

Chapter 13: Science and Faith Together

1. Ulrich Hildebrand, "Das Universum—Hinweis auf Gott?," *Ethos: Die Zeitschrift für die Ganze Familie* 10 (October 1988): 10. The quote cannot be found in Heisenberg's published works, and Hildebrand does not declare his source.

2. Werner Heisenberg, "Scientific Truth and Religious Truth," *CrossCurrents* 24, no. 4 (1975): 463–73, https://www.jstor.org/stable/24457901.

Appendix D: Discovering Darwin's Letter

1. Richard Dawkins, *A Devil's Chaplain: Reflections on Hope, Lies, Science, and Love* (New York: Mariner Books, 2004), 69.

SY (SEYMOUR) GARTE, PhD in biochemistry, has been a tenured professor at New York University, Rutgers University, and the University of Pittsburgh, division director at the Center for Scientific Review of the National Institutes of Health, and interim vice president for research at the Uniformed Services University of the Health Sciences. He is currently visiting professor of pharmacology and toxicology at Rutgers University. He has published more than two hundred peer-reviewed scientific papers and four books.

Dr. Garte is a fellow of the American Scientific Affiliation (ASA) and serves as vice president for the Washington, DC, metro chapter of the ASA. He was a member of the board of advisers of the John Templeton Foundation and the board of directors of WesleyNexus, and he has consulted and blogged for the BioLogos Foundation. He has published articles in *Perspectives on Science and Christian Faith* and elsewhere and is the editor in chief of *God & Nature*. Dr. Garte has given presentations on the intersection of biochemistry, evolution, and theology at several conferences devoted to science and Christianity. Dr. Garte became a Christian later in life and is now the lay leader of the United Methodist Church in Rockville, Maryland, and a lay delegate to the Baltimore-Washington Annual Conference of the United Methodist Church.